BOTTOM LINE BELIEFS

Smyth & Helwys Publishing, Inc.
6316 Peake Road
Macon, Georgia 31210-3960
1-800-747-3016
©2009 by Smyth & Helwys Publishing
All rights reserved.
Printed in the United States of America.

The paper used in this publication meets the minimum requirements of
American National Standard for Information Sciences—
Permanence of Paper for Printed Library Materials.
ANSI Z39.48–1984. (alk. paper)

*Library of Congress Cataloging-in-Publication Data*

Brown, Michael B., 1949–
Bottom line beliefs: twelve doctrines all Christians
hold in common (sort of) / by Michael Brown.
p. cm.
ISBN 978-1-57312-520-8 (pbk. : alk. paper)
1. Theology, Doctrinal—Popular works. I. Title.
BT77.B855 2008
230—dc22
2008054149

# BOTTOM LINE BELIEFS

## TWELVE DOCTRINES ALL
## CHRISTIANS HOLD
## IN COMMON
### (SORT OF)

## MICHAEL B. BROWN

# DEDICATION

To the people of Centenary United Methodist Church in Winston-Salem, North Carolina, who were so loving in goodbye . . .

To the people of Marble Collegiate Church in New York, New York, who have been so gracious in hello . . .

And to Page, who supported and empowered me in both places.

# CONTENTS

# INTRODUCTION

When considering the global Christian family, we are quick to realize that diversity and disparate opinions are the rule. We are not just one church. Even a quick glance at historical theological disciplines introduces us to Roman Catholic tradition, the Greek Orthodox tradition, the Anglican tradition, the various Reformed traditions, Anabaptist traditions, Moravian traditions, and many more. Global Christians are anything but one lockstep church.

Approximately thirty percent of the world's population call themselves "Christian." That totals just over two billion people who live in almost every nation on every continent on earth. Precise numbers are impossible to come by, but experts agree that there are thousands of denominations and sects within the Christian family, each a bit different from all the others. From cherished dogmatic principles to behavioral codes to manners of dress, the differences between Christian denominations are profound. Likewise, within every particular denomination, matters of biblical interpretation, sacraments, church governance, ordination, human sexuality, soteriology, eschatology, and even Christology are sources of significant debate and disagreement.

Among the readers of this book are some who call themselves "Baptists." Historically, that is a meaningful and honorable name. But what kind of Baptists? There are Southern Baptists, Cooperative

Baptists, American Baptists, Free Will Baptists, Missionary Baptists, and a hundred other kinds as well.

When I served as student pastor of a United Methodist church in eastern North Carolina, immediately across the street from our congregation was a Primitive Baptist church. Both our churches were small and did not have air conditioners, so in summer we left the doors and windows open. Thus, those who were members of my congregation had a choice: they could listen to the sermon I was preaching or the one being preached across the street. They both came in at about the same decibel level. We always concluded our services by noon, whereas our neighbors concluded theirs about 2:00 p.m. I would usually exit my church about the time our neighbors had taken an intermission for lunch on the grounds. There I was, a student preacher who looked all of fourteen years old in my robe and stole, and there they were gazing at me as if I were from another planet.

I had friends in seminary who were student pastors of American Baptist churches. Their theology, style of worship, and pulpit attire were precisely the same as my own. Are you a Baptist? There is nobility in that. But what kind of Baptist are you?

Another says, "I am a Lutheran." Again, there is nobility in that. But what kind of Lutheran are you? Are you Evangelical Lutheran Church of America (a traditional and centrist denomination), or are you Lutheran Missouri Synod (a more conservative denomination)?

"I am Presbyterian." Again—noble. But what kind of Presbyterian are you: Presbyterian Church USA, Presbyterian Church of America, or Orthodox Presbyterian?

"I am an Episcopalian." Wonderful! Does that mean Anglican? Are you Evangelical Episcopal? Southern Episcopal? African Methodist Episcopal Zion? American Diocese? Diocese of Kenya?

As I said, I belong to the United Methodist Church. There are twenty-seven Methodist denominations in America. Not every one is United Methodist. There are Free Methodists, Pentecostal Methodists, AME, AME Zion, CME, Wesleyans, the Church of the

Nazarene, and on and on. Even within one's own particular theological heritage there are variations.

Narrow the focus even further. Forget the global church or even a particular denomination. Within one local congregation, whether it is Baptist, Methodist, Presbyterian, Catholic, or whatever, diversity is still the rule.

On Sunday morning wherever you worship, the odds are that you occupy a pew with members of your own congregation who disagree with you about subjects varying from the Virgin Birth to the sacraments to whether or not the Bible is the literal or the inspired, poetic word of God. In one's own house of faith, people are seldom of a single mind.

In short, the Christian church does not even remotely resemble a great ocean liner moving along a charted course to transform the world. At best, it is a flotilla of thoughts and practices that sometimes defies anyone trying to determine a method to its madness or any evidence of a common destination, let alone a common map for getting there.

Given the disparate nature of church, one is tempted to ask, "If Christians can't agree about anything significant, how should they expect to evangelize non-Christians into such a dysfunctional family?"

This question, though frequently posed, is inevitably flawed. As Arthur Van Seters has pointed out in "Dilemmas in Preaching Doctrine: Declericalizing Proclamation," "far from being powerless or meaningless, doctrinal engagement has the potential to restore brokenness and invite newness."[1] There are, in fact, a number of principles that all Christians of all traditions hold in mutual appreciation. They make up the common map for our faith journey. Any study of those principles has the poignant potential to which Van Seters referred.

This book addresses several such principles that are bedrock. Though individual denominations, congregations, and Christians may argue about how to interpret these particular doctrines, all Christians accept and affirm some interpretation of them as central and vital to the practice of the faith. About each of these principles we say, "I believe in that. It is dear to me. It is nonnegotiable. It is indispensable to my faith." Though we may differ on the nuances of each of these doctrines, we still confess that they are central to our understanding of Christianity. They are the *bottom line beliefs* that form the corpus of this work and of our shared Christianity—the cohesive theological issues that serve as our common ground.

The treatment of each theme in this book's chapters will be biblical, theological, historical, sermonic, and sometimes anecdotal. Upon closing the Bible after her first reading of it, St. Therese said, "I see myself there reflected." Hopefully in the consideration of the chapters to come, you will find your faith reflected and, perhaps, even strengthened.

Read. Ponder. Discuss with someone you trust. And then, to quote Fred Craddock, "Chase your own rabbits."

Any book of theology is ultimately a personal journal for the reader. Thus, may you find in these pages whatever is personally best for you.

## Note

1. Arthur Van Seters, "Dilemmas in Preaching Doctrine: Declericalizing Proclamation," *Journal for Preachers* 17/3 (1994): 31–40.

# CHAPTER 1

# GOD AS CREATOR

The things that separate us become the hot topics of our faith conversations: baptism, salvation, apostolic succession, sexual orientation, divorce, abortion, women in ministry, the role of faith and politics, biblical interpretation. The list is long and only grows longer as the church continues to reinvent itself. Somehow, though, in the midst of our diversity, there are a handful of common threads that keep holding us all together.

Obviously, the best idea always seems to be for one to begin at the beginning. For people of faith, the beginning is the concept of God as Creator.

Admittedly, the effort to define God as "Creator" adequately is beyond any human effort. In his book *This Sunrise of Wonder*, Michael Mayne (former dean of Westminster in London) cites Isaac Bashevis Singer, the Jewish novelist. Singer once said that commenting on the Creator is like asking a worm crawling through a volume of *War and Peace* to comment on Tolstoy as a writer. There he sits, chewing on a single letter of the alphabet, totally unaware of the sweep of Tolstoy's genius.

Yet, we people of faith continue our efforts to comment, to interpret, and to understand. Even acknowlging our limitations, we can do nothing less than seek for meaning about life and the One who threw it into motion. Our search for meaning and understanding returns to the beginning of things and to the One who set it all in motion. Every Christian believer will affirm, "In the beginning God created the heavens and the earth" (Gen 1). That is a fundamental statement of our faith. All Christians agree to that. We do not agree about *how* God did it. We simply agree *that* he did it.

An old dictum from the world of philosophy says that wherever you see a watch, you can be certain there is a watchmaker. People of faith paraphrase this, saying that when we observe creation, we can be certain that it demands the existence of a Creator. We look at a universe that is far too intricate, too complicated, and too well designed to be an accident. Creation gives the appearance of being "thought out."

That is our statement of faith. We believe that there is a God back of Creation, back of the universe, back of the world, back of human life. How God did it remains a topic about which we do not all agree. We simply agree *that* God did it.

Some people believe God created the world in six days and rested on the seventh day. Some believe God began an evolutionary movement of our earth and that we are still evolving. But the believers in either group would say, "I am convinced that behind the watch is a watchmaker. Behind creation is a Creator."

Some people believe in Intelligent Design of the universe, while others believe in the Big Bang theory. Interestingly, that is not a biblical debate. The Bible never enters that argument. Furthermore, if it did, the Bible could embrace either side. My father used to tell me, "People who believe in the Big Bang must find affirmation in the first chapter of Genesis. There's a verse that says, 'God said, "Let there be light," and suddenly (Bang!) there was light.'" The Bible simply does not argue or even speculate about how God created the earth. It rather attests *that* God created the earth.

Often persons begin their study of this sacred story by staking out positions on data: How long did it take God to create the world? Were Adam and Eve created simultaneously, as the first chapter of Genesis teaches, or did Adam come first, as the second chapter teaches? How does one reconcile the two? Such thinking does not take into account the fact that the Bible is not a science text. It is, rather, a book of faith. (This will be more fully explored in chapter 6, "The Role of Scripture.")

The Bible relates oral traditions that existed for centuries before anyone wrote them down or even had the capacity to do so. Within all the twelve tribes of Israel, people told their stories. Eventually those stories were compiled, with the result that sometimes two accounts of the same story, placed side by side, were slightly different. The differences become problematic only when one reads Scripture asking *how*. Scripture is not designed to answer that question. Instead it addresses the theme *that*. Its stories from the oral traditions agree *that* God created—that behind the watch, there is a watchmaker.

From the most ancient texts to the modern day, believers have come together around the common faith in a Creator. "In the beginning, God created the heavens and the earth." We honor that belief, and in it we find hope. That hope has to do with sensing that we matter. As Christians, we believe this universe, this world, and our lives are not accidental. We were created by God, according to a Divine intent, and that ascribes an inherent sense of dignity and worth to every life.

Occasionally all of us must wonder if God is always pleased about what he created. When I was a child, my mother often asked a disturbing question of me. Entering my room, she would ask rhetorically, "Did you make this mess?" First of all, it was my room. Second, Dad was at work. Third, I was an only child. Fourth, her question indicated that she was not responsible for the mess, which effectively narrowed down the answer. I always knew her question was merely a prelude to what would come next. "Did you make this mess?" she would ask, and no matter how I responded (or even if I remained silent), she would order, "You've got ten minutes to clean it up."

Sometimes as we observe life on this planet, it is impossible not to wonder if God doesn't occasionally ask, "Did I make that mess? Is this what I created? Surely this is not what I had in mind."

There are wars and rumors of wars, hunger and homelessness. Three hundred people are blown up by a car bomber in a public square in Baghdad. Nineteen hundred a week are murdered in Darfur. A senior at Virginia Tech kills thirty-two students and professors before turning the gun on himself.

In business life, in family life, in politics, and too often even in church, when God sees how people treat and mistreat other people, surely he must wonder, "Is this what was intended? Who made a mess out of my creation?"

Deep whispers of faith suggest that God looks at life from a broader perspective than we do. Mortals are captives of the contemporary moment. We can read and dream about what went before and what might yet come, but in reality we exist within rather narrow parameters. We are captured by what we experience in the brief span of our lives. What Cesar Milan says of canines (*The Dog Whisperer*) may be true of mortals: we are primarily creatures of the moment. Therefore it is easy for us to look at the world and say, "It is all terrible! It is all tragic!"

God, though, observes from a broader perspective, much as Boethius taught when contemplating his idea of "the eternal now." God sees the total picture, the world from the innocence of creation to the moment of redemption, and, therefore, though it is spotted and stained, he can still view it and say what the authors of Genesis wrote: "It is good."

Occasionally that broader perspective breaks in on us. I spent twelve wonderful years serving churches in two cities in the Appalachian Mountain range. One was a university community, and the other was a bustling city rich in arts and tourism. In each place I cherished autumn. Something happens to a person in autumn in the mountains. For most of the year you become used to your environment. You are surrounded by the beauty until you no longer see it as the tourists do. It's just where you live. You go to work, deal with your family, pay the bills, fix the car, eat the meals, go to sleep, get up, and go to work again, almost immune to the ambiance of your world.

But then, every autumn, comes peak season, that time when the mountains begin to glow with leaves that are fiery red, yellow, and orange. And you experience an unexpected and wonderful moment of epiphany. While you are about the business of living your daily life, not thinking or feeling anything grand, suddenly you look around at your environment and say, "My Lord! How did I miss this—the grandeur of these mountains, ablaze with color as if some magnificent artist created something on a global canvas that nobody else could create?" In that moment, when you look at the beauty of creation and are absorbed by it, it becomes almost impossible to deny the reality of a Creator. You find yourself saying, "In spite of all the tragedies and trials of this world, it is still good."

My son Adam was at the coast recently and sent me a text message from his cell phone. When I opened it, I found that he had forwarded a picture. I was at work in an office in the middle of a city. But he was at a beautiful place called Fort Fisher. It was sundown when he sent the picture. It was of a long expanse of seashore and a magnificent body of water with waves kissing the sand. The sun was setting beyond the horizon of blue waters, and the sky was painted pink and gold. Pausing from my hurried, busy, too-often-thoughtless life, I looked at the picture and experienced a divine interruption, an epiphany in which I confessed, "My Lord! This gorgeous creation simply demands the existence of a Creator! When you see a watch this exquisite, there is somewhere a watchmaker." And I found myself saying, "It is good." Edna St. Vincent Millay captured the heart of this faith in her sonnet "God's World," which concludes with the septet:

> Long have I known a glory in it all,
> But never knew like this;
> Here such a pattern is
> As stretcheth me apart. Lord, I do fear
> Thou'st made the world too beautiful this year:
> My soul is all but out of me—let fall
> No burning leaf; prithee, let no bird call.[1]

You and I live in a troubled world, a world of hunger, homelessness, and pain. Whether one dwells in Palestine, Iraq, or in an American inner-city ghetto, one deals with excesses of fear and abuse. But even in the midst of that, there are people who labor to make the world different, a more beautiful and better place, a holier and more sacred place, and who honor the lives of all who are wounded and weary. When we see them, it is like epiphanies, like mountain colors or ocean waves breaking in and reminding us of the Creator. God's perspective enables us to see those people, even amid life's dark and arid places, and to say, "It is good."

Simon Bolivar (for whom the country Bolivia was named) led Peru to independence from Spain in 1824. Suddenly Peru was a nation. They were their own independent people. Bolivar was the architect of their newfound freedom. Predictably, they went to him and asked him to become their first president. He was their George Washington. But Bolivar answered, "No, I am a liberator, not a governor. My work is to bring freedom to people."

The people desired to offer him at least some reward, some symbol of their gratitude. So they gathered up a million pesos and took them to Bolivar, saying, "This is our gift of thanks."

He said, "I will accept it on one condition—that I can match it with funds from my own estate, and all of it will be used to purchase freedom for three thousand people in Peru who are still living as slaves. If you will allow me to use your money to set them free, I will receive it."

"It makes no sense," he said, "to set a nation free unless all its people experience freedom."[2]

In a moment like that, amid the pains of revolution and the reality of slavery, surely God must have looked down upon this one noble crash of the waves upon the sand and said, "It is good."

In the midst of human pain, there remain reflections of the redemption yet to come. From time to time, even upon this planet of the fallen, some human spirits stand tall and say, "I will spend my life for the sake of others."

Every time we give ourselves away in some loving fashion, or every time we witness someone else stand tall in willingness to help, to heal, to listen, to rescue, or to love, surely God says, as we should say, "It is good."

Individual Christians may vary widely on *how* God did it, but Christians all agree *that* "in the beginning God created the heavens and the earth." Regardless of *how*, we come together and assert that behind the watch is a watchmaker, behind creation a Creator. We also all agree that when that Creator is honored and obeyed, it is good.

## Notes

1. Edna St. Vincent Millay, "God's World," from *Renascence and Other Poems* (1917). Available online: www.bartleby.com/131/4.html (accessed 8 January 2009).

2. Herhard Masur, *Simon Bolivar* (Albuquerque: University of New Mexico Press, 1948), 86-89, 233.

## Questions for Discussion

1. How does the concept of a Creator galvanize people of faith?

_____

_____

_____

_____

_____

2. Discuss how "creationism" or "evolution" can be faith-based explanations of the origin of life.

_____

_____

_____

_____

_____

3. Name specific realities that strengthen our personal concepts of God as Creator.

_____

_____

_____

_____

_____

4. Discuss the realities of (a) evil and (b) beauty as they relate to your concept of God as Creator.

_____

_____

_____

_____

_____

# CHAPTER 2

# THE CENTRALITY OF JESUS

The late Lewis Grizzard used to tell of Joe, a man approaching midlife who felt less and less confident about himself. Overly concerned with physical attributes, he was depressed by his male pattern baldness and his overfed, underexercised potbelly. The last straw came when he asked a woman coworker out on a date, and she all but laughed at him. "That does it," he decided. "I'm going to start a whole new regimen."

So, said Grizzard, Joe began attending aerobics classes. He started working out with weights. He changed his diet. He got a nose job, a face lift, and an expensive hair transplant. He got his teeth capped, glittering white. In six months, he was a different man. Again, he asked his female coworker out, and this time she accepted.

When the big night arrived, Joe was beside himself with excitement. All dressed up for the date and looking better than he ever had, he stood on her porch poised to ring the doorbell when a bolt of lightning struck and knocked him off his feet. He was launched off the porch. He plastic nose and cheek implants melted. His muscle implants were dislocated. His new hair curled in smoke from the top of his head.

Lying on the ground, stunned and shaken, he turned his eyes toward heaven and said, "Why, God? Why now? After all I've been through, how could you do this to me?"

From above, there came a voice: "Sorry, Joe. I didn't recognize you."[1]

As noted from the outset of this work, sometimes denominations look so different from one another (and even individual Christians within the same church are so dissimilar) that you would not recognize us as being related at all. But there are a handful of bottom line beliefs that make us family. Central to those beliefs is the status of Jesus within the community of faith.

A woman I know often brags that her church is a "theological rainbow." It is made up of liberals and conservatives, Republicans and Democrats, charismatics and social justice advocates. She happily reports that they all attend the same Sunday school classes, all work side by side on Habitat for Humanity houses, and all love and take care of one another. When telling me about her church, she said, "We differ on so many things, but we all get together around Jesus."

Assuming what she said to be true, then hers is a New Testament model church. One such church was the congregation in Philippi. In the book of Acts, Luke presents a cross section of its constituents. There was a woman named Lydia who sold expensive linen and was a significant financial player in the city. There was a Roman jailer who was your garden-variety, middle-class government employee. And there was a local fortuneteller who was, in fact, a slave, an inhabitant of the lowest strata of society.

Lydia was from Asia. The jailer was from Rome. The fortuneteller was a hometown girl. All were wanted and welcomed in the same church. Though they were socially, educationally, culturally, and economically almost indescribably disparate, they shared a commitment to the life, teachings, and centrality of a man from Nazareth. They all got together around Jesus.

In the beginning we considered the wide variety of perspectives and theologies within the Christian church, and how denominations and individuals within the same local congregation may seriously disagree about everything from the Virgin Birth to the sacraments to how we interpret Scripture. That being the case, it is still true that all Christians agree that the central element of our experience of faith is the man Jesus. If that were not the case, we would not be part of a movement named after him—*Christ*ians.

Admittedly, we vary on what he means to us and how to interpret him, but every thinking person at least confesses that *Jesus is a man who transformed human culture.*

Over the course of the centuries, the Christian church has been the genesis of such things as public health care, hospitals (which originally existed within cathedrals where injured soldiers were brought for rest and recuperation), nursing (primarily by the nuns in those cathedrals), public education, women's rights, child advocacy laws (particularly dating back to the social justice commitments of John and Charles Wesley in eighteenth-century England), counseling (originating in the confessional), social services, etc. All came into existence as programs of Christ's church.

*Some see Jesus as a "rabbi" who taught the ultimate ethical system for life within community.* Early American deists (like Thomas Jefferson and Benjamin Franklin) who did not believe Christ was Messiah, that he performed miracles, or that he was raised from the dead, still encouraged Americans to live as Christians. This they did out of a belief that the healthiest way for people to treat one another within a new country was based upon Jesus' principles of ethics.

Even today we hear the statement, "Jesus was a great teacher." He must have been, considering that the lessons he taught and the principles he espoused live on in the fabric of every nation in Western culture.

One needs to look no further than the Sermon on the Mount to see the practical power of his teachings. Matthew's Gospel uses those teachings to inaugurate Jesus' rabbinic ministry. Luke does the same with his version called the Sermon on the Plain. Each is a compilation of "Jesus quotes"—things the disciples recalled that he said during his life and ministry. Matthew's expanded version is like a mini-Bartlett's, establishing quote by quote the ethic of Christ. Certainly, one does not have to be a Christian to sense the depth of that ethic or its universal applicability.

Just consider, for example, two statements at the beginning of that collection. Jesus says, "You have heard that it was said to the men of old, 'You shall not kill; and whoever kills shall be liable to judgment.' But I say to you that every one who is angry with his brother shall be liable to judgment; whoever insults his brother shall be liable to the council, and whoever says, 'You fool!' shall be liable to the hell of fire" (Matt 5:21-22). In one clear statement, Jesus articulates how sophisticated people commit murder and get away with it—simply by demeaning others. No longer did they take up swords and shields as did the itinerant Hebrews during the exodus, but they knew (as we do) how to destroy another human effectively. Out of self-interest, people decided to critique publicly, to level insults, to paint others as being "foolish" (thus not to be taken seriously), to resort to whispers and innuendo, and thus to curtail or even kill altogether the reputation and influence of their neighbors. Jesus recognized and taught that this behavior is unacceptable, almost as serious as physical assault.

During the 2000 presidential campaign, a candidate who had won in New Hampshire suffered a smear attack in a key southern state. Supporters of his opponent circulated a rumor that the leading candidate had questionable sexual morals and, as a married man, had illicitly fathered a biracial child. In short, they hit two of the key nerves that resonated with those on the religious right: human sexuality and racism. The candidate about whom the rumor was spread was innocent of the charges, but the resulting damage caused him to lose the primary and eventually the nomination. His desire to be of public service was effectively killed by slander leveled at him by his opponent's supporters. Jesus' ethic speaks to sophisticated murderers who subtly destroy the lives of others without ever resorting to gun or knife.

"You have heard that it was said, 'You shall not commit adultery.' But I say to you that every one who looks at a woman lustfully has already committed adultery with her in his heart" (Matt 5:27-28). Here Jesus communicates a sexual ethic that goes deeper than mere physical desire and instead addresses the desire to use, own, or possess another individual for personal gain. It is not simply the act of fornication that he condemned, but the desire within the heart to objectify someone else for personal pleasure, thus dehumanizing that person in the process.

On and on these quotations go, one by one establishing a new ethic that was based not merely on action but also on attitude. Thus did the new ethic of Jesus demand more than the Law of Moses brought down from Sinai. And, whether one believes in Jesus as Messiah or not, whether one is or is not a person of faith, the ethical principles he espoused provide a clear, sound, and reasonable system for interpersonal relationships. It is how we perceive others that determines how we treat them. Jesus' Sermon on the Mount is, in the end, about how we perceive and value our neighbors.

*Some see Jesus as a personal presence.* He challenges us in our daily decision-making. He comforts us in times of crisis. He confronts us at work or school or home, asking us, as he did Matthew, to "Rise up, and follow" (Matt 9:9). He is intensely personal and involved in our human lives.

Perhaps the bottom line of faith in a living, ever-present Messiah is the effect it has on our courage. Luke 24 describes the experience of Cleopas and a friend on the road from Jerusalem to Emmaus following the crucifixion. Apparently they had been friends and followers of the Nazarene teacher and believed he was the awaited one who would restore the future of Israel. However, on Friday all those dreams had crumbled in dust at the foot of the cross. So they limped back to Emmaus with heads and hearts hanging, shrouded in grief and tears.

Luke says, "As they made their way, Jesus himself drew near and walked with them." Initially, "their eyes were kept from recognizing him." (Or perhaps, in fact, "they couldn't believe their eyes.") Who could blame them? If you see someone die on Friday, you don't expect to see him walking the road to Emmaus on Sunday. But after they had spent some time in the presence of that stranger who drew near and walked with them, "their eyes were opened, and they recognized him. And they said to one another, 'Did not our hearts burn within us when he walked with us on the road?'"

Those men in Emmaus had moved from despair to joy, from defeat to strength, from tears to laughter, from fear to hope, and from grief to faith. All this had occurred because of a mysterious and unexpected living Presence with them on life's highway.

Some years ago, a three-year-old was trapped under a building that caved in on a farm in West Virginia. Emergency personnel gathered as TV crews looked on and filmed. It took several hours for rescue workers to dig their way to the child, who, as far as they knew, might already be dead. They worked slowly, afraid that if they were too aggressive, the rubble would collapse again. As it turned out, the boy survived. He was trapped in a small oxygen capsule where logs laid over one another like a lean-to. One arm was broken, and he was bruised, but when they finally dug him out he was remarkably calm and apparently not frightened at all.

His grandmother was present at the accident site the whole time. When workers emerged with the child, she kept saying, "I begged Jesus to protect you. I knew he would." Later, the child, who was only three, said, "Jesus talked to me while I was buried in the wood. I told him I was scared, and I wanted out, and my arm hurt. And he kept saying, 'I'm going to stay right here with you, and you are going to be just fine.'"

We can interpret that however we like, as a small boy's imagination or merely as wishful thinking. But in the mind of that three-year-old, Jesus was a personal presence in a time of crisis, and in that presence the child found the comfort and courage to survive.

Many believe that Jesus is a living presence in our lives—confronting and challenging, to be sure, but also a source of divine comfort and courage. They believe he is "with us always" (Matt 28:20), as he promised before the Ascension, and that he holds us close in arms of love when otherwise we would fall.

Transformer of culture. Ethical Teacher. Personal Presence. However one understands him, for Christians Christ is central to who we are and what we do. In some wonderful, mystical sense, we all get together around Jesus.

## Note

1. Lewis Grizzard, *My Daddy Was a Pistol, and I'm a Son of a Gun* (New York: Villard Books, 1986).

# Questions for Discussion

1. In what ways has Christ transformed human culture?

_____

_____

_____

_____

_____

2. How does our understanding of Jesus inform and affect our concepts of right and wrong?

_____

_____

_____

_____

_____

3. Discuss theological and/or anecdotal support of Jesus' words, "I will be with you always" (Matt 18:20).

_____

_____

_____

_____

_____

4. What does it mean to be "Christocentric" (a) as an individual, and (b) as a faith community?

_____

_____

_____

_____

_____

# CHAPTER 3

# JESUS' RESURRECTION

Despite the often pronounced and profound differences among denominations, local churches, and individual Christians, there are a handful of bottom line beliefs that provide cohesion, beliefs that we all embrace and that make us one family in spite of our differences. Perhaps none is more obvious than the belief that death did not end the life or influence of Jesus. We may argue about various theological dogmas from the Virgin Birth to the gifts of the Spirit, but all Christians believe the words of the Apostles' Creed, that Jesus "was crucified, dead, and buried. (And) on the third day, he was raised from the dead." A bottom line belief for all Christians is a belief in the resurrection.

Of course, what Christians believe about the resurrection varies widely. My best friend in college was a young man studying to become a Southern Baptist minister. We double-dated. We were the starting backcourt on the Religion Department's intramural basketball team. I was the best man in his wedding. But, when it came to matters of doctrine, our opinions were rarely the same. Phil, who is a distinguished professor of Biblical Studies at that same university, used to say, "As friends, let's just agree to disagree. You see it your way, and I'll see it God's way."

Within the Christian family, though we agree on the fundamentals, what we believe about them may vary widely. Such is certainly true for the various ways Christians interpret the resurrection. The bottom line is simply that all Christians agree that something miraculous occurred.

There are four ways of interpreting the resurrection: as an apparition, as the sense of Jesus' nearness that is a normal part of the grief process, as the reality of an ongoing influence that death could not undo, or as a physical phenomenon. Each understanding is different. Yet the proponents of all four interpretations would affirm, "Yes, I believe in the resurrection. It validates my belief in Jesus."

Some interpret the resurrection as *more of a spiritual than a physical phenomenon*, almost as if Jesus were an apparition. Such an understanding is neo-Docetic, and despite the fact that Docetism was deemed heretical centuries ago, its influence and broad level of acceptance remains undeniable even today.

Television's Travel Channel frequently devotes Friday night to ghost stories. Shows like *The Most Haunted Hotels, The Most Haunted Campuses,* and *The Most Haunted Cities* air one after another. Many of us find these shows fascinating. Recently a show dealt with the ghosts of Gettysburg. For those who believe in ghosts, that little town in Pennsylvania is considered one of the most haunted cities in America. People report spending nights in bed-and-breakfast hotels that were once battlefield hospitals and say they suddenly saw Civil War soldiers in full attire standing at the head of the stairs. They could see them, but they could also see through them. Just as suddenly, the soldiers would vanish or disappear through a wall.

Many first-century Christians believed that was how Jesus existed after the resurrection. He was alive, and he was seen, but he was not actually flesh and blood. Those who believe this appeal to a story from John's Gospel where the disciples are gathered together in a locked room, and the Risen Jesus simply walks through the door and appears in their midst. It is difficult for a flesh-and-blood human to walk through a closed door, but for a ghost, it would be no challenge. Or proponents of the ghost theory quote a story from Luke where Jesus appeared to the men on the road to Emmaus.

Then at the table in their house, he suddenly vanished from their sight—again, a rather ghostly thing to do.

Another way of interpreting the resurrection is that Christ's followers in the days after the crucifixion merely *felt his nearness with them*. Not infrequently we hear someone say, usually within the first few months of a major loss, "I could feel his spirit with me," or "I could sense her presence in the room." That feeling does not ordinarily extend past the first few months of grief, but we hear it expressed all the time. A grieving wife reports walking into her den for the first time following the funeral service and feeling as if her former husband were still sitting in his rocker. A grieving husband reports suddenly catching a whiff of his deceased wife's favorite perfume, as if she had just walked by. Those are physical manifestations of emotional grief. Some believe that the disciples, in the primary stages of grief, experienced "lingering presence"—a natural phenomenon that led to their reports that Jesus was still alive and with them.

A third way some have interpreted the resurrection is simply to say that the cross could not kill Jesus' *ongoing influence in the world*. There are those who suggest that following Jesus' death, every time the disciples returned to a place where they had been with him, they remembered him so vividly that it was as if he were still there. That feeling inspired them to stand up, to survive, and to move forward. So, in that sense at least, he actually *was* still alive for them or, in fact, through them.

Jesus' teachings, his principles, and the lives of discipleship exhibited by his followers all survived in spite of the cross. There are those who say that Jesus lives on *through* the people who started the Christian movement and keep it going. Paul put it this way: "It is no longer I who live, but Christ who lives through me." In fact, the Greek actually reads, "It is no longer I who live, but *Christ who lives me*!" (Gal 2:20). Jesus' teachings and influence were far too powerful to be silenced by death.

Bishop Kenneth Goodson was recognized as one of America's greatest preachers of the twentieth century. He was also a courageous denominational leader in the Deep South during the days of desegregation. Toward the end of his career, Goodson spent several years as bishop-in-residence at Duke University Divinity School, where he had a powerfully transformational influence on the students who studied under him.

Bishop Robert Morgan told me about an event in the lives of some of those students who had graduated and were serving as pastors. When news of Goodson's death reached them, a number of those former students from several states away formed a car pool and drove to North Carolina to pay their respects. At the funeral home for the evening family visitation, those young men and women approached Mrs. Goodson. One of them said to her, "As long as we are alive, Ken Goodson will never die!"

Many believe that Jesus' disciples were similarly committed. As long as they were alive, they kept his memory alive, and still do even today. They feed the hungry and house the homeless. They build schools and hospitals. They counsel the depressed and preach sermons. They write books and serve Communion in remembrance of him, and as long as they do that, he lives on through them. Everything he stood for continues to challenge and change the world.

Albert Schweitzer was invited to lecture at the University of Chicago Divinity School. A number of academic dignitaries went to the train station to welcome the world-famous clergyman/musician/surgeon. Straining to catch sight of him, they were surprised to see Schweitzer serving as a volunteer porter for an elderly woman. Walking beside her, he was carrying her luggage to a waiting area. She was small and frail and apparently incapable of lifting the weight of her bags. So Schweitzer, naturally and without fanfare, simply picked them up and carried hem for her. One of the scholars who observed him remarked, "He wrote of the search for the historical Jesus. He could have found him merely by looking in the mirror."

Many interpret the resurrection as the Christ-like witness of those who day by day keep his ministry alive and serve the world in his name.

Finally, there are many traditionalists among us who accept the idea of *the bodily resurrection of Jesus.* In John's Gospel, Jesus says to Thomas, "See my hands and my feet. Place your hand in my side. See that it is I myself" (John 20:27). At another place, beside the lake, he cooked breakfast and ate with the disciples (John 21:12-15). Those are indications of a physical presence, and not some mere vision or apparition. This is the primary understanding of resurrection embraced by Christians throughout the centuries.

Those who interpret the resurrection in the traditional sense appeal to two convincing arguments: (1) the biblical witness and (2) the experience of the martyrs.

As for the biblical witness, Matthew, Luke, and John all include stories of the physical resurrection of Jesus, while only Mark, the first Gospel, does not. Also, Paul talks about it, at one point saying that he could name "five hundred others to whom Jesus appeared" following the resurrection (1 Cor 15:6). It is possible to get a few people to help you pull off a hoax. It is not reasonable to think you could convince five hundred to do so. The witness of the people who were present following Jesus' death is a strong argument supporting the traditional interpretation of his bodily resurrection.

Then there is the experience of the martyrs. Obviously, and understandably, some respond to the biblical witness by saying, "Of course your Bible tells those stories. That is your unique book of faith. It is supposed to tell your story—as the Koran does for Islam or other books do for other faith systems. Give me something more credible than that." That is a fair argument. If more support is needed, many find compelling the fact that in the days following the death of Jesus, when the Roman Empire began trying to destroy Christianity, thousands of believers chose to suffer martyrdom rather than to deny the fact that Christ was alive.

Consider, for example, a man named Polycarp, who was bishop of Smyrna. Roman officials asserted, "Cut off the head, and the dog will die. If we can get Polycarp to deny his faith, the believers who follow him will let go of their faith, too, and the movement will end." Polycarp was therefore arrested and taken to Rome.

During his imprisonment, Roman officials virtually begged him to deny his faith publicly. They even told him he did not have to mean his public recanting of the faith. He could simply say it, and they would let him go. Polycarp steadfastly and stubbornly refused.

Finally he was taken to the coliseum, tied to a stake, surrounded by straw, and threatened by death with fire. One last time they sought to convince him. "If you will just deny your belief in the resurrection," they said, "we will untie you and send you home."

Polycarp answered (and his words became the rallying cry of Christians throughout the Roman Empire): "Eighty and six years have I served him, and he has done me no wrong. How then should I blaspheme my King who saved me?"

His captors lit the fire, not knowing that they were setting ablaze a new epoch of evangelistic zeal among his followers.

One rarely endures something like that "on a hunch." One does not risk one's life for a rumor. Thousands of brave martyrs died rather than deny their belief in the resurrection, and that convinces many of us that they didn't merely *think* it happened. They *knew*.

## Questions for Discussion

1. Contrast "Docetism" with the traditional idea of a physical resurrection of Jesus.

_____

_____

_____

_____

_____

2. Is the validity of Jesus' ministry dependent upon a traditional interpretation of his resurrection? Explain your response.

_____

_____

_____

_____

_____

3. In what ways does our influence on others provide us with a form of life after death?

_____

_____

_____

_____

_____

4. Discuss the influence of Jesus in the personal resolution of grief experiences.

_____

_____

_____

_____

_____

# CHAPTER 4

# THE HOLY SPIRIT

A little girl was curled up in her bed after her grandmother read her a fairy tale. Before drifting off to sleep, she asked, "Grandma, do all fairy tales begin with the words, 'Once upon a time'?" Her grandmother answered, "No, sweetheart. Most fairy tales begin with the words, 'If elected, I promise . . .'!"

Every campaign season causes us to think like Grandma. Whereas most TV political ads preach to us about the dramatic differences between opposing candidates (and how one side is patriotic and the other isn't, or how one side is intelligent and the other isn't), in truth, most candidates have a lot more in common than they have differences. So it is with Christians. Often we focus on our differences when, in truth, the most important ideas and principles we all hold in common.

Take, for example, our commonly held belief in the Holy Spirit. Admittedly, what we believe about the Spirit differs. When some speak of the Spirit, they are talking about Pentecostalism (e.g., things like seeing visions and speaking in tongues) and referring to the story in Acts where "the Spirit came upon them with tongues of fire" (Acts 2:3). Those readers are convinced that the story emphasizes the importance of spiritual gifts such as glossolalia.

Others read the same story and say, "No, it doesn't mean that at all." They are not part of Pentecostalism but of Evangelicalism,

emphasizing a different verse from the same pericope: "And everyone heard in their own native tongue" (Acts 2:11). In other words,
as they read the story, the point is simply that God's salvific message
is for all people who will hear and believe.

At end of the day, wherever we wind up in the debate about the
*works* or *manifestations* or *gifts* of the Spirit, we all believe in the *reality* of the Spirit. And the Bible is clear about what that means.

There are two primary biblical understandings of Holy Spirit.
One is from the Old Testament use of the Hebrew word *Ru'ha*. The
word means "breath," and its employment theologically refers to the
life-giving breath of God, the clearest contemporary illustration of
which is probably the act of artificial respiration when one person
literally breathes his or her life into another, making that person
come alive. Thus, the Holy Spirit can be defined as "God *in* us."

Medical science confirms that our physical essence is to a great
extent determined by what we put into our bodies. Any thinking
person finds it intriguing to consider what we choose to ingest. Over
the course of a lifetime, the average person eats sixty thousand
pounds of food, which is roughly the equivalent of the weight of ten
elephants. An article in a 2006 edition of *New York Magazine* considered extreme diets and how longevity may be related to existing
on a diet of two thousand calories or less per day. The article suggested that we truly are what we eat. One contributor, an alternative
nutritionist, said that the human body is designed to live far longer
than most of us do *if* only we put the right things into it. The author
cited a man in New York City who is six feet tall, weighs one hundred and fifteen pounds, and exists on a diet of things like raw
vegetables, barley, and seaweed. Do this, he suggested, and you can
fully expect to live to be one hundred twenty years old. There are
those of us who would offer the counterpoint that if all you can eat
is barley and seaweed, who would want to live to be one hundred
twenty years old! Still, it is true that what we put into ourselves
determines what we ultimately become.[1]

The Bible suggests that there is a spiritual correlative to that
physical principle. What we put into our souls determines what we

ultimately become, and so Scripture frequently talks about inviting God's Spirit into our lives. Often it uses breath imagery. In Ezekiel there is the story where the dry bones are connected and finally come to life. It happens when "the wind of God's Spirit blows upon them" (Ezek 37:1-11). In John's Gospel, Jesus likens the Spirit to "the rush of a mighty wind" and says that it "blows where it will" (John 3:8), meaning that if God lives in us, he often leads us to go places and do things we would never have done on our own. When God is in us, we become something different than we have ever been before.

Ru'ha—the breath of God, the life of God, *in* us.

The New Testament concept of the Holy Spirit shifts focus somewhat from God's breath to his presence: "God *with* us." One traditional understanding of "God with us" is that of a *convicting presence* (as in the voice of conscience). A Native American legend tells of a boy on a mountain who saw a shivering rattlesnake. Drawing his bow and arrow, he was about to shoot the serpent when it raised its head and began to plead for mercy. The snake asked the boy to carry him to the foot of the mountain so he could survive. If left upon the mountaintop he would freeze to death, but at the foot of the mountain he would thaw out and live.

The young man replied that he could not carry a rattlesnake. It would bite him, making him ill, perhaps even taking his life.

"Oh no," answered the snake. "I will not bite you. You will be the hero of the village, probably the next chief. They will admire you for being the only person who can hold a rattlesnake and not be bitten."

The idea was appealing. It fed the boy's ego. So he agreed. Placing the snake within the warmth of his blanket, he carried it gently to the foot of the mountain and laid it in the warm earth.

Immediately, the snake coiled and bit him. Falling to the ground and writhing in pain, the young brave shouted, "Why did you do that? Why did you break your word?"

As it slithered away, the reptile answered, "You knew I was a snake when you picked me up!"

"Thou shalt." "Thou shalt not." Such is the voice of conscience, the whisper of God present with us, warning us, and protecting us not only against evil but also against ourselves. It is a voice that warns us about what to pick up and what to discard.

"God with us" has also traditionally been interpreted as a *comforting presence* (as in the voice of love). My mother died on Monday, December 22, 1986. She was buried on Christmas Eve. In the lovely little church where I was then pastor, we always observed a service of Holy Communion on Christmas night. People would come at the end of that long and happy day to receive the Lord's Supper and give thanks. I was their minister and felt I had to be there that evening, despite the loss I had suffered. Yet, amid the pain of grief, I felt I had little to offer.

It was Christmas—the first Christmas in my life without my mom—and I had a four-year-old son who didn't understand why she hadn't been sitting beside the tree that morning. My father, the victim of a stroke only three months earlier, was living with us. He had suffered the loss of his health, his job due to the illness, and his wife of forty-eight years. It was all I could do to go to the church, prepare the table, and try to think of something to say.

But it was a moment I will never forget. As the worshipers came to the altar and knelt, and as I reached out to them with bread and juice, one by one they grasped my hands. They smiled. They wept. And as each group stood to leave the altar for their seats, one by one they reached across the altar, took me in their arms, and hugged me. Never before had the meaning of "the communion of the saints" been so clear. That night the Spirit of Christ came to me in my brokenness and cradled me in the arms of his church. I knew beyond doubt that God was with me and with all our family. We experienced his comforting presence through his people.

A third traditional understanding of "God with us" is that of *a calling presence*. It is the Spirit of God with us that invites us to journey with him. As described in the biblical story of the call of Matthew when Jesus said, "Follow me, and he rose and followed"

(Matt 9:9), so all of us who open ourselves to a divine nearness experience, in time, a divine invitation, a sense of calling.

One of the many legends surrounding the life of St. Francis of Assisi illustrates how persons of faith are asked to do that which we would not ourselves have chosen. Francis, it is told, was terrified of leprosy, and understandably so. Thus he avoided lepers intentionally and consistently. One day while riding his horse through the country, he rounded a curve and came upon a ragged leper standing in the roadway. The man was so shabby and pitiable that somehow Francis's fear gave way to sympathy. His sympathy gave way to epiphany. He saw Jesus in the sufferer. Suddenly he remembered the words of Christ: "In as much as you have done so unto the least of these, my brothers and sisters, you have done so likewise unto me" (Matt 25:40).

Francis, frightened of contact with lepers and worried about contracting the disease, dismounted from his horse, removed the leper's clothing, bathed him in a nearby stream, then gave the man his own fine garments and put upon his body the leper's rags. He had been called to serve, to sacrifice, and to love, even when loving was dangerous and made him personally vulnerable.

Like Francis, many fear contact with people infected with HIV/AIDS. Many fear speaking about faith in public. Many fear sharing their financial resources with anything remotely approaching reckless abandon. Many fear the ostracism, if not the outright persecution, that may come from challenging the government when it is immoral. Many fear leaving a lifestyle of comfort to embark upon a lifetime of ministry. But the truth remains: God consistently calls believers to do things we would not have chosen on our own. It is God's prerogative. How we respond reveals the extent to which we are open to his presence with us.

God *in* us. God *with* us. Those are the bottom line interpretations of Holy Spirit as contained and proclaimed through the Old and New testaments. And whereas Christians often debate the nature of the Spirit's gifts, manifestations, or works, we all agree that

God's presence is experientially verifiable, and that presence is our clearest understanding of his Spirit.

## Note

1. Julian Dibbell, "The Fast Supper," New York Magazine (23 October 2006). Available online: www.nymag.com/news/features/23169/ (accessed 8 January 2009).

# Questions for Discussion

1. In what ways do we sometimes confuse "the gifts of the Spirit" with the Holy Spirit itself?

_____

_____

_____

_____

_____

2. In what ways could the Holy Spirit affect or influence one's behavior?

_____

_____

_____

_____

_____

3. Discuss the Holy Spirit as "God in us."

_____

_____

_____

_____

_____

4. Discuss the Holy Spirit as "God with us."

_____

_____

_____

_____

_____

# CHAPTER 5

# THE DOCTRINE OF THE TRINITY

When one speaks or writes of "the Trinity," the mind immediately thinks of occasions like Trinity Sunday or the familiar lyrics "God in three persons, blessed Trinity" (from the hymn "Holy, Holy, Holy"). Just as quickly, the questions form: "What the heck does that actually mean?" "How many gods do we believe in? Is it just the one God, or when you add Jesus and the Holy Spirit, do you wind up with three gods instead?"

Athanasius said that the doctrine of the Trinity is "wholly incomprehensible and by us embraced." Many feel he got the "incomprehensible" part right.

Theologically, many Christians have no idea how to comprehend this doctrine because sometimes it almost sounds like a confession of faith that there are three gods competing with one another—or, at least, operating more or less like a C.E.O, C.O.O., and C.F.O. But if we believed in three gods we would be "polytheists." Christians have always been "monotheists" (which means "believers in one God").

The language of Matthew's Gospel confirms that. Jesus instructed his followers to "go into all the world making disciples, and baptizing in the name of the Father and the Son and the Holy Spirit" (Matt 28:19-20). In the Greek (as in the English) three gods (or three anything) would have required a plural noun. In other words, it would have read, "Go ye into all the world making disciples, and baptizing in the *names* (plural) of the Father and the Son and the Holy Spirit." Instead, the Greek says, "Go ye into all the world making disciples, and baptizing in the *name* (singular) of the Father and the Son and the Holy Spirit." It may be a small thing, but it is a critical thing. The Greek word specifically designates one person, not three—one single God who is revealed or understood in three different ways.

Think of it this way: You are one person. Some people primarily know you as *Parent*. One individual primarily knows you as *Spouse*. A couple of other people primarily know you as *Child*. You are one person, but you are known, understood, and interpreted in a variety of ways.

So it is with the doctrine of the Trinity. There is one God, but we see him in a variety of ways dependent upon our individual perspective. Some people think *theologically*, so their primary understanding of God is *Creator* (the one who builds and manages the whole universe).

Others find that concept too big to get their arms around. They think *relationally*. They need a personal God, a God with a face. They need to listen to his words, to determine what he thinks and what he's like. They primarily think of God as *Jesus* (the person who most clearly revealed God to us).

Still others think *emotionally*. They feel, they dream, and they want to sense nearness, attachment, and mystery. They primarily understand God as *Spirit* (*paraclete*: the divine presence who is with us "always, even unto the end of the world").

The point is that however one most clearly identifies or understands the Deity, we are always talking about one God who is interpreted or understood in different ways.

Karl Barth, in his *Christian Dogmatics*, referred to God as "Revealer, Revelation, and Revealedness." In other words, God, who knows us, seeks likewise to be known by us. He seeks to reveal himself to us, that a relationship may be formed. He is thus "Revealer." God did this by sending Jesus, the "Revelation" of God. Jesus was not God, but God was present in and revealed through him. William Barclay, in his *Commentaries*, said that all we can know of God is what we see revealed in Jesus. In the human Jesus, God showed the world his own nature. The Holy Spirit is the ongoing awareness and understanding of that divine revelation, the "Revealedness" of God. The Revealer presents himself over and over, and we are empowered by relating to and understanding that which has been revealed.

Again, the bottom line is that we are always talking about only one God who is understood, interpreted, or revealed in three different ways.

Some will reply, "This does not make sense for one reason, and that reason is biblical. The Bible indicates that Jesus prayed to God. If we worship Jesus, and if we worship God, and if Jesus prayed to God, then there have to be at least two gods, right?" In a word: No. Orthodox Christian doctrine has never taught that. Instead, for two thousand years it has taught that Jesus was a man who lived to be about thirty-three and was so righteous, stainless, and virtuous that God was able to live in him more fully than he ever had in anyone else. Paul attested to that by writing, "God was in Jesus, reconciling the world to himself" (2 Cor 5:19). Jesus was a man; Christos was God's Spirit that dwelled within him and was revealed through him.

How can this principle be adequately illustrated? Suppose you were to be shown an empty soda bottle and asked what it is. You would no doubt reply, "It's an empty bottle." It is a container. It is something that holds soda. But, if that same container were filled with cola, and you were asked what it is, you would answer, "It's a Coke or a Pepsi" or whatever. The bottle is just the container. It is the cola that matters. The cola is revealed and made available through the container. Jesus, the man, was the container through whom the Christos (or God) was revealed and made available to the world. But the miracles, the power, the preaching—all of that was God working in and through the form of a man.

That is what the Trinity means: one God (only one) whom we know, interpret, and understand by looking at him from three different perspectives.

At some point, of course, another question arises: "So what?" What difference does any of this make in our lives in the world? Consider two responses to that question.

Because God lived in the man Jesus, *he understands what we feel and experience.* The New Testament says, "He was tempted in all things, as we are" (Heb 4:15). Properly understood, that means he experienced all things as we do. Thus, when we pray to God, he does not listen as one who has no clue what we are talking about. Instead, God listens as one who has been there, as one who has walked where we walk and has felt what we feel.

Several years ago I sat in a surgeon's office, facing a rather involved operation. Predictably, I was worried about what my recuperation would be like, what I could or could not do, how much pain I would experience, how long it would be before I could drive again—all the normal worries people face before surgery. The physician must have sensed my anxiety, for he stopped speaking clinically, and he said to me, "I can tell you exactly what to expect. Here's how it was for me when I had the same surgery." Suddenly I heard him in a new way, and my confidence in him deepened. He knew what I was going through because he had been there himself.

When we cry out to God from the darkness of our lives, from guilt or grief, from sin or sadness, from despair or depression, he knows what we are going through because he has been there himself. By living inside the human Jesus, the Bible says, God experienced all things as we do. Because of that, God listens with an understanding ear, so that when we fear wrath and judgment, instead he offers mercy and grace.

Second, because God is Holy Spirit (a comforting presence), *whatever we face in life, we do not face it alone.* Not only has he walked where we walk, but he chooses to walk the same road all over again beside us, for us, with us. That was the promise at the ascension in Matthew 28: "I will be with you, always, even unto the end of the world" (or as is paraphrased in some modern versions, "even when it feels like your world is ending").

When Jeremiah Bailey suffered a head injury in an automobile accident at age six, his mother (who was also injured) would hobble down the hospital hall each night on her crutches and sleep in a recliner near his bed. Before sleeping, she would sing to him his favorite song, "The House on Pooh Corner," she would say the Lord's Prayer, and she would kiss him good night. He never moved. He never opened his eyes. He never made a sound.

When she recovered sufficiently to be discharged, she would still come to her son's room every night. Most nights she still slept in the recliner, but sometimes she would stay until 10:00 or 11:00 and then return to her home. Either way, every night she would sing his song, pray the prayer, and give him a kiss.

Jeremiah did not respond much for four full months. Then one morning, he opened his eyes and said, "I'm hungry." Just like that, he was awake and alive again. The doctors, nurses, and physical therapists asked if he were aware of anything during those four long months in a coma. The little boy answered, "I knew Mommy was here. She sang to me and said prayers, and that stopped me from being afraid." Something about the presence of a loving parent with him in the darkness gave him the calm and the courage required to survive.

Because God is a loving Presence (Spirit), he is with us in the darkness. "I will be with you always, even unto the end of the world." The knowledge of his presence gives us the calm and courage required to survive.

How many gods do we believe in? Just one—the one God who made us, who took on human form for a while to show us what he is like, and who promises that wherever we go and whatever we face, he will be "with us always." I described it once this way:

One God made known in many ways,
Whose presence with us never strays,
Holds fast and dear the ones He made,
And walks beside us all our days.
And walks beside us all our days.

# Questions for Discussion

1. What does it mean to you to worship God as Trinity?

_____

_____

_____

_____

_____

2. In practice, do you think most Christians are essentially "polytheists" or "monotheists"? Explain your response.

_____

_____

_____

_____

_____

3. Why might a person believe that Jesus "understands what we feel and experience"?

_____

_____

_____

_____

_____

4. If there is only one God revealed in three ways, how do you interpret Jesus' practice of prayer?

_____

_____

_____

_____

# CHAPTER 6

# THE ROLE OF SCRIPTURE

A collector of rare books encountered an acquaintance who told him he had just thrown away an old Bible he found in a dusty box. He happened to mention that Guten-somebody-or-other had printed it. "Not Gutenberg?" gasped the collector. "Yes, that was it," the man replied. "You idiot!" said the other. "You've thrown away one of the first books ever printed. A copy recently sold at an auction for a million dollars!" "Oh, I don't think this book would have been worth much," replied the man. "Some guy named Martin Luther had scribbled all over it in the margins."

A bottom line belief all Christians share is in the inestimable worth of the Bible, no matter who printed it or scribbled in its margins. In a fundamental sense, every Christian is a biblical enthusiast. From fiery Pentecostals to cerebral UCC's (United Church of Christ), all of us would agree that the Bible is the word of God, and therefore it must be true since God is truth.

All of us within the Christian family believe that the Bible is our ultimate book of faith and practice, a record of many of God's dealings with our forebears, a handbook for daily living, and a guidebook for successful living. What we believe about it and how we interpret it may differ, but we all embrace it as the most important document ever written. And through it, God continues to

speak clearly and powerfully today to those who will simply read
and listen.

That being said, how believers read, listen to, and interpret holy
writ varies widely. Some people believe that every single word in the
Bible is literally, historically, scientifically, and geographically true.
They even have their own bumper sticker: "God said it. I believe it.
And that settles it."

I sometimes envy biblical literalists. Life for the theologian
would be much simpler if we could take codified faith documents at
face value. But over the course of years in the serious study and practice of Christianity, some of us believe that if we try to interpret the
Scriptures literally, we encounter more roadblocks of rationality than
if we interpret it as God's inspired word.

At first blush, one assumes a literalist does not have to worry
about how to interpret anything. A literalist would not, for example,
appear to have any worries about putting a text into context, figuring out what those people back in some little village two thousand
years ago actually believed and practiced, or discerning what meaning they assigned to various words that may be different from the
way those words are currently interpreted.

But even a literalist cannot long avoid the issue of whether
Hebrew or Greek texts have been accurately translated into English
and how to deal with certain phrases that can mean two different
things at the same time. For example, when we read of the disciples
in the boat at night being rocked by the winds and the waves, the
Greek says that Jesus appeared and the sea grew calm. However, a
word is used that meant two different things. It says, "He walked *on*
the water." The same Greek word also means "He walked *toward* the
water." Which is it? If I am a literalist, I am trapped as I try to figure
that out. But if I interpret the Bible as God's *inspired* word, then I
read the story and discover truth—that Jesus came to them and
brought peace in the midst of their storms, even as he does for us.

If I am a literalist, I am challenged to come to terms with the
fact that in the King James Version of the Bible there are six hundred and eleven mistakes (nowadays we would call them "typos"),

places where some scribe late at night, deprived of sleep, wrote a word or phrase that was clearly incorrect. Consider one as an example. In Matthew's Gospel of the Palm Sunday account, it says "Jesus came riding on a donkey and on a colt, the foal of a donkey" (Matt 21:5). That was to fulfill an Old Testament prophecy about how the Messiah would enter God's city. A donkey was an emblem of peace. If a king entered someone's city on a stallion, everyone knew he came as a warrior to conquer. If he entered the city on a donkey, everyone knew he came as a friend to make peace. The Old Testament added that the donkey would be a newborn, "a colt," symbolizing not only peace but also purity. Thus, the Old Testament prophecy was that the Messiah would come "on a donkey, a colt, the foal of a donkey." It seems perfectly reasonable that the person who copied Matthew's document from Greek to English accidentally added the word "and," thus indicating that Jesus rode two animals into Jerusalem at the same time (which might have explained why so many people came out to watch!).

The longer one devotes one's self to being a scholar of Scripture, the more he or she realizes the difficulties inherent in interpreting the Bible literally. In truth, if I am a literalist, I am in trouble by the time I reach the second chapter of the Bible's first book. Genesis gives us two different creation stories. In chapter 1, "male and female he created them" *at the same time.* In chapter 2, God made man first and later took a rib out and used it to create woman. If one takes the Bible literally as a book of history and science, then he or she faces issues in Genesis 1–2 because these chapters tell one story in two completely different ways. If you see these verses, however, as a collection of oral traditions all simply seeking to articulate that "in the beginning, God created the heavens and the earth" (Gen 1:1), then there is no problem at all. Two variations of one story have simply been included in an ancient document, side by side. Neither refutes the central proposition of the story. Rather, each tells it in a slightly different way, like the accounts of the same event as told in two different newspapers. The essence is identical, but there are variations in the particulars.

If some wish to deny women the right to have leadership roles in church or to become ordained ministers, they can take texts out of Corinthians and say, "See! Paul said that women cannot speak in church, and if they have questions, they have to go home and ask their husbands" (1 Cor 14:35). Paul does say that to the Corinthians. However, in almost every other letter he wrote, Paul bragged about the women who were leaders in the church—evangelists, teachers, preachers, and even persons in whose homes the church met for worship. (When the infant church met in a person's home for worship, that person was the acknowledged head of the local congregation.) How does one reconcile those things if every word of the Bible is to be taken literally?

On the other hand, what if you read Corinthians with an understanding of Corinth? Then you realize that in Corinth, people worshiped, for example, in places like the temples of Aphrodite and Isis, and those places were led by women priestesses. Men were prohibited from teaching. Only the women fulfilled that role. Practices like temple prostitution were the rule, and even human sacrifice was not a distant memory. So when Paul started a new church in a city with that kind of culture, he had to make sure the converts did not bring their old practices along with them.

Paul told the Corinthian Christians that they would do things differently—in fact, they would do them in a way opposite from how their religion had been practiced all their lives, even to the point that women, always before the leaders in the pagan temples of the city, could not even speak in this new church. No sacrifices. No temple prostitution. None of the former things. Instead, this was a new church practicing faith in a new way. In Philippi and Thessalonica, apparently, those issues did not exist in a similar fashion. Nor were those the issues facing the infant church in Rome. So in those cities Paul welcomed women as leaders. The Bible, to make sense, has to be read with an understanding of the context of the persons to whom it was written, the persons who wrote it, and the issues facing them in their specific towns and villages in that particular day and age.

Shortly after moving to the city where I currently live, the door-bell rang early one Saturday morning. Answering it, I found a young man with a Bible and religious tracts in his hand. He wanted to ask me some questions.

First he asked if I were "saved," and I told him I was. Then he decided to find out if that were really the case, so he asked his two plumb-line questions. "Have you surrendered your life to Jesus?" I answered quickly: "Yes, I have. Otherwise, I would surely be in some other line of work!" He then moved on to his bottom line: "Do you believe the Bible is the literal word of God?" I said, "No. I believe it is a story of faith that includes poetry and metaphor, and it contains God's truth."

That was all it took. I had apparently failed his test. He began explaining to me that I could not be "saved" if I did not believe in and practice God's word literally. (Obviously he had no idea of the Greek word for "salvation," which is *soteria* and does not refer to doctrinal rigidity or even to one's destination in the afterlife, but simply means "to become whole.")

When he stopped for air, I asked, "Are you married?" "Yes sir." "Do you have children?" "Not yet, but we hope God will bless us with children." "If that happens, will you rear them according to the teachings of the Bible?" "Absolutely!" I continued, "Word for word, with no exceptions?" "Yes, I will!" Then I asked, "Then what will you do with a word from the Deuteronomic Code that says if your child is disrespectful, you are to take him outside the city walls and stone him to death? Will you do that to your child, or is it possible that you don't actually take the Bible literally after all?"

He had no answer, and rather quickly rushed off to ring the bell next door, hoping, no doubt, that the people who lived there would be less adversarial.

Our culture has matured in the past three thousand years. We don't sacrifice animals or children anymore. Back then, they did. We no longer consider women to be property (the Hebrew word is "chattel"). Back then, they did. We do not discipline our children by stoning them to death if they are disrespectful. If we did that, a friend suggested, there would not be a single teenager alive in America today!

Instead, we read the Bible as a guidebook, a document that espouses principles of faith, and whose specific words are often hyperbole or metaphor, not literal instructions at all. We recognize that the harsh-sounding word from the Old Testament law merely illustrated the life-or-death urgency of teaching young people to respect others in authority. It didn't actually encourage parents to murder their children, and there is absolutely no indication that the verse was ever literally applied.

The truth is, when we read the Bible literally, we often get mired in data and miss the truth. In a church I served many years ago, a Bible study group spent several weeks reading the book of Jonah, only to determine that Jonah must have been swallowed by a sea grouper because a whale's mouth is not large enough to ingest a human. They even requested that I make that announcement to the church. (I replied that I really did not want to take credit for their research, so perhaps their data should be disseminated in some other way.)

Those folks spent weeks with Jonah and missed the entire point of the book. T. S. Eliot described such persons by saying, "We had the experience, but missed the meaning." Who cares about the fish? Who cares if there was a fish, or, for that matter, even a Jonah? The story is a Hebrew *midrash* (parable), and it points us toward deep truths about God's will, our response to God's call, the price we pay when we try to flee from him, and the miracles he can work when we simply do what he asks us to do. But those Bible study members missed every bit of that because they were intent on figuring out what kind of fish could actually swallow a human being!

Frequently on television there are documentaries about Noah's Ark and whether or not its remains actually sit on Mount Ararat. Again, who cares? Who cares if there was an ark or a Noah? It doesn't really matter. (I have always had serious misgivings about anyone who had a chance to swat the two mosquitoes, forever blessing the rest of us, but refused to do so.) If we wish to take the story of Noah literally, then what do we do with questions like these: How big would a boat have to be to get two of every living creature on it? How would the North American buffalo have gotten over to Israel to board the boat? The simple truth is that, if we read the Noah story as a piece of history or science, we miss the story.

The story is a piece of rabbinic *midrash* about our sin and God's judgment. It is about our faithfulness and God's providence. It is about God's concern for all life, not just human life—about being cleansed and given fresh starts and new beginnings. Yet some people waste their time trying to figure out how the boat was built or what mountain it landed upon and miss God's truth revealed in the story.

This chapter began with the thesis that the Bible is our handbook of faith and practice. In truth, our varied approaches to biblical interpretation nothwithstanding, the original thesis may be more hypothesis than fact. Put another way, the question may not be *how* Christians read Scripture, but rather *if* we give it particular attention at all. Is it a document with transforming impact, or has it been relegated to the role of a curious relic or a leather-bound centerpiece for the coffee table?

An old proverb accurately states, "The Bible has not been practiced and found wanting. Instead, the Bible has been found difficult, and therefore is rarely practiced."

## Questions for Discussion

1. Discuss the differences between belief in the Bible as the "literal" Word of God and the "inspired" Word of God.

_____

_____

_____

_____

_____

2. What role does the Bible have in the practice of faith?

_____

_____

_____

_____

_____

3. What is the difference between "data" and "Truth"?

_____

_____

_____

_____

_____

4. Is the Truth of God still being revealed in post-biblical times? Explain your response.

_____

_____

_____

_____

_____

CHAPTER 7

# THE NECESSITY OF GRACE

You and I are not good enough. We simply are not. Will Rogers used to say, "We are all ignorant, just about different subjects." The same thing is true about abilities. In one area, I'm not good enough. In another, you aren't.

As much as I wish I could be a soloist in the church choir, I'm not good enough. Forget being a soloist; I'm not good enough to be a member of the choir. I'm not even good enough to put sheet music in folders for the choir. I simply do not have musical gifts.

When I was a boy, I wanted to be a first baseman for the New York Yankees. As a Little Leaguer, I had a good glove and a good bat. But, as I got older, the pitching changed. Little League pitchers threw fastballs and change-ups. That's all they could do. Either one I could smack out of the park. But as they grew, they learned to pitch curves. I could see curves. I just couldn't hit them. So I wound up as a good fielder who couldn't hit well. As far as a career in base-ball was concerned, I wasn't good enough.

I was a fairly decent high school basketball player. If we had had three-pointers back then, I would've been a star. I could shoot. I still can. There were, however, things I couldn't do, like jump high and run fast and defend well. I was too short to rebound. I couldn't handle the ball effectively. You get the picture. I would have loved to play college basketball, but I wasn't good enough.

A friend said to me some time ago, "My dream is to have my own show on the Food Network, to be the next Rachael Ray. The only thing stopping me is that I'm a terrible cook!" In short, in that area, she's not good enough.

Historically, the Christian church has taught that no one is morally or spiritually good enough to earn their place as a member of Christ's family. How did Paul put it? "All have sinned and fall short of the glory of God" (Rom 3:23). The early church fathers (particularly John Calvin) taught a doctrine called "Original Sin," indicating that the day we are born, we are already sinners, already morally separated from God and goodness. That doctrine remains a core belief in numerous denominations today, not the least of which is the Roman Catholic Church.

In some old cemeteries in parts of New England, rock walls separate burial spots. On one side of the walls are graves of babies who died after baptism. On the other side are graves of babies who died before baptism. The walls were built as an attempt to assist Jesus after the Second Coming in determining which children should be resurrected and which others left behind. Though this is an extreme idea and seems unpalatable to the modern mind, it gives evidence that throughout history virtually all Christians have consistently agreed that fundamentally we are not good enough.

Of course, some of us think we are at least better than most of the others. There's an old joke that is known by all and told on all—Baptists, Catholics, Assemblies of God, Episcopalians, Methodists, name your poison! It goes like this: Someone dies and goes to heaven. St. Peter is giving him a tour. He takes him down one street and says, "The Lutherans live here." On the next street he says, "The Presbyterians live here." On the next, "The Baptists live here." On and on it goes, until he comes to a corner and tells the man, "Take off your shoes, tiptoe, and do not say a word while we walk down this street. The _____s live here, and they think they're the only ones in heaven!" (Insert whatever denomination makes you laugh the most, and the joke works the same.) Deep down, all Christians have always known it is only a joke, for we have almost universally agreed that none of us is really that good, and, if any of us gets to heaven, it will be for a reason other than that we deserve it.

What would that reason be? Again, hear the words of the new covenant: "By grace have you been saved through faith, and this is not your own doing. It is a gift of God" (Eph 2:8). One of the bottom line beliefs of all Christians is the absolute, undeniable necessity of grace.

Arguably the greatest biblical illustration of this doctrine is Jesus' wonderful story of the prodigal son (Luke 15). The younger son took his share of his inheritance and wandered into a "far country" where he "wasted his goods in riotous living." Then "he came to himself," went home, and begged his dad to let him be part of the household again. His older brother, who had stayed home and worked the farm and never disobeyed a single command to break his daddy's heart, was livid when the younger brother returned. He was particularly angry that his dad seemed so happy and forgiving about it. In fact, the father had said to the servants, "Let's kill the fatted calf and have a party, for this my son was dead and is alive again. He was lost and is found." That did not sit well with the older brother, so he refused to go to the party. When his dad came out to ask why, he erupted. "You never killed a fatted calf for me! You never threw a party in my honor, even though I stayed right here and served you without a word all this time while this son of yours spent your money on harlots!"

Two observations: The older son had crossed out the younger brother. He had divorced him from the "family." He did not say "my brother," but "this son of yours." Second, where did he get his information that his brother had spent his inheritance on harlots? Did the younger brother phone the older or send him e-mails from the far country? "Having a wonderful time! Wish you were here!" How did he know what the young man had done with the money? He did not know. He could not know. He was guessing. As Ellsworth Kalas suggested in *Parables from the Back Side*, the elder brother was probably thinking, "If I had that much money and went out of town, that's what I would do with it!"[1]

Upon careful reading, it becomes obvious that the father in this story did not have only one sinful son. He had two. One was outlandish and in-your-face, off to some orgy of Saturday night sinning. But he had another son, an older son who was bitter, judgmental, and unloving and, as such, just as sinful as his younger sibling.

The father in the story made room in his heart and home for both boys. To one he said, "Put shoes on your feet and the family signet ring on your finger, and let's have a party." To the other he said, "Everything that is mine is yours."

Why did he treat two bad boys in such a generous fashion? Because he loved them. Not because they were particularly lovable, but because they were his. And to him, home was not home if his boys were not there.

That, said Jesus, is how God loves us. It's all about grace.

Therefore grace, properly understood within the biblical framework, is closely akin to the experience of homecoming. A sense of belonging within a given family unit is not something to be purchased. It is essentially a gift from the acknowledged hosts of the home.

The poet Robert Frost said, "Home is the place where, when you have to go there, they have to take you in" whether you've been good or not.[2] That is grace as illustrated in Jesus' lovely tale about a father who provided that gift to two undeserving children.

A United Methodist bishop told of the time he ran away from home as a teenager. Two days later, tired and hungry, he made his way back to his parents' house. As he turned the corner and started up the sidewalk toward the front door, he spotted his father sitting in a rocker on the porch. He stopped in his tracks, not knowing how or if he would be received. All his father said was, "Go wash up, son. It's supper time."

Bishop Kenneth Goodson told a similar story about a farmhouse in the Pennsylvania Dutch country. An upstairs bedroom had a light burning in the window day and night. Goodson asked someone at a local general store why the light was left burning constantly. He was told that the young daughter who lived there had run away under the cover of darkness several years before. She had been neither seen nor heard from since. Her parents left the lamp burning, in their words, "so that if she ever decides to come home, her room will have a light on."

Frost was right. And so was Jesus. Grace isn't about being bad or good. It's about having a home.

Even a cursory reading of the New Testament reveals the undeniable importance of that doctrine in the lives of the biblical saints. Mary the mother of Jesus was, in all likelihood, an unwed girl between the ages of twelve and fourteen, an embarrassment to her family, and perhaps shunned by her community (thus explaining her retreat to Elizabeth's home). She had done nothing remarkable and lived in the forgettable town of Nazareth (note Nathanael's commentary on that village: "Can anything good come out of Nazareth?"; John 1:46). When an angel appeared to Mary at the annunciation, she cowered. Who wouldn't have?

But despite her lack of credentials, she was informed that she had been "chosen." She had not earned the honor of bearing the most important baby in the history of the world. She had been chosen. She rightly confessed, "He that is mighty has done unto me great things" (Luke 1:49). A sense of "family" was given to Mary, not earned by her. She was the recipient of grace.

Simon Peter was rough, rugged, and profane. James and John were inflammatory, not to mention that at one point they appear to have been maternally dominated egotists. None deserved to be part of the inner Twelve. They were chosen to be members of the family.

A powerful illustration of this principle is found in the story of the Gerasene demoniac, which is related by all three of the Synoptic Gospels. When the deranged man was healed and restored to his right mind, he did not ask to return to his village. He did not desire to go back to the family of his birth. Instead, he said to Jesus, "Please, let me go with you." Home, for him, was not so much a place as it was a relationship. He had found his sense of "home" in

Christ. That was the result of nothing he himself had done, but rather of the graciousness of the One who had performed the exorcism that freed him from his suffering.

St. Paul, history's greatest interpreter of the life and ministry of Jesus, was arrogant, unforgiving, and an accomplice to the murder of the first Christian martyr. His credentials did not warrant apostleship. But, as Luke reported in the book of Acts, somewhere on the highway leading to Damascus, Paul was chosen. By grace he was brought into the family.

Ernest Hemingway wrote a story about a Spanish father who decided to reconcile with his son who had run away to Madrid. Now remorseful, the father took out an ad in *El Liberal* newspaper: "Paco meet me at Hotel Montana noon Tuesday. All is forgiven. Papa." Paco is a common name in Spain, and when that dad went to the square he found eight hundred young men named Paco waiting and hoping for their fathers.[3]

That's us—children who want someone to love us even when we have ignored them, someone to forgive us even when we have betrayed them, someone to accept us even when we have rejected them, someone to embrace us even when we have resisted them, someone to claim us even when we have disobeyed them, someone to bless us even when we have denied them, and someone to take us back home even when we have given away our birthright—like the father of the prodigal son who opened his heart and house to his child not because the child was worthy but because he was his son and home was not home without him.

In some cultures the word "grace" means "to long for." The way you would long for a spouse or a lover whose romantic embrace says things words cannot express. The way a hungry person would long for something to eat. The way a parent or grandparent longs for the sight or sound of a child or grandchild during the holidays. The way an injured person longs for good health. The way an imprisoned person longs for freedom. The way the father of the prodigal son longed for his child to come home. The way Paco's father longed for someone who was lost, and the way those eight hundred Pacos longed to be found and loved again.

Grace is one of our bottom line beliefs. All Christians who have ever read the New Testament and who understand the meaning of the cross, liberal or conservative, high church or house church, Catholic or Pentecostal or anything in between, at last stand on the same ground, acknowledging that God loves us in spite of ourselves. He longs for us with a holy passion. Therefore, "By grace are we saved through faith, and this is not our own doing. It is a gift of God" (Eph 2:8).

## Notes

1. J. Ellsworth Kalas, *Parables from the Back Side: Bible Stories with a Twist* (Nashville: Abingdon Press, 1992).

2. Robert Frost, "The Death of the Hired Man," from *North of Boston* (1915); available online: www.bartleby.com/118/3.html (accessed 8 January 2009).

3. Ernest Hemingway, "The Capital of the World," from *The Fifth Column and the First Forty-Nine Stories* (New York: Scribners, 1938).

# Questions for Discussion

1. According to the Parable of the Prodigal Son, membership in God's family is dependent on what?

_____

_____

_____

_____

_____

2. Discuss the meaning of "unconditional love." Is there anything you can do that will cause God to stop loving you?

_____

_____

_____

_____

_____

3. The Ephesians 2 text indicates that grace is completely God's initiative and is not based on our behavior. Discuss that idea in relation to the idea of "universal salvation."

_____

_____

_____

_____

_____

4. Can grace be rejected? Explain your response.

_____

_____

_____

_____

_____

# CHAPTER 8

# DISCIPLESHIP AS A RESPONSE TO GRACE

In the preceding chapter we considered the doctrine of grace as a bottom line belief shared by all Christians. All traditional Christians agree that whatever our denomination, whatever our doctrinal heritage, through our own merit none of us is "good enough" to earn a place in God's kingdom.

As noted in that chapter, a perfect biblical illustration of that principle is Christ's story of the prodigal son in which the father, who represents God, loves both of his sinful boys: the prodigal who immersed himself in "riotous living" *and* his older brother who was both begrudgingly faithful and a judgmental jerk.

The older brother came to mind when I saw a bumper sticker on a car in front of me. It simply read, "Lord, deliver me from your followers." Immediately I thought of those who resent the happiness of others and are quicker to judge than to love. The opposite sentiment is expressed in yet another bumper sticker that reads, "I was sinking deep in sin, wheeeeeee!" That brings to mind the prodigal, a person whose self-indulgence was equivalent to hedonism. The theological beauty of the story, of course, is that the father forgave them both because he loved both. "By grace are you saved through faith, and this is not your own doing. It is a gift from God" (Eph 2:8).

The question may then be asked, "If membership in the kingdom has nothing to do with our behavior, then why behave? Why not just join forces with the prodigal and party our way right into heaven?" That question opens the door to examination of another bottom line belief: the nature of discipleship.

Every Christian denomination, without exception, believes that Jesus meant business when he said, "If anyone would come after me, let him deny himself and take up his cross and follow me" (Matt 16:24). Every denomination believes in the absolute, undeniable importance of discipleship.

But why? If we are made part of God's family purely by grace, and if our behavior doesn't earn us a place in his kingdom, then why does our behavior matter at all?

Two reasons: First, discipleship is *a mark of our relationship with God.* Theologian Paul Tillich's concept is true, that our lives of discipleship are an indication that we have accepted the fact that we have been accepted.

Consider politics as an example. Suppose you choose to be a Democrat. You register to vote and sign up as a member of that party. You don't have to pass a test. You don't have to *do* anything. The Democrats want you as a member and accept you with open arms. But then you proceed in every election to vote a straight Republican ticket. That would show that you did not respond to their acceptance—that although they accepted you, you rejected them.

The same would be true of a person who registers Republican and consistently votes Democrat. You would not accept the fact that you had been accepted.

Neither political party requires a new member to sign an oath of loyalty, to be good enough, or to swear undying allegiance till death. They accept with open arms, free of charge. But it is possible, having been freely accepted and embraced, to reject that acceptance.

A person who chooses to live a self-absorbed, immoral life has rejected the God who accepted him. That person holds grace at arm's length. He or she remains in "the far country."

Living a good, decent, caring, loving life does not make God love us. God already loves us. Instead, it shows that we have responded to that love. We have accepted the fact that we have been accepted.

A young man named Ian McDonald returned from a tour of duty in Viet Nam. He had been reared in a good and also strictly religious home. Following dinner one evening after his return, his father asked the son to join him in the study. Once there, the dad said, "I have read of a place in Saigon called 'the meat market,' a red light district where soldiers on R&R visited prostitutes. It has been a source of such worry to me, wondering if you went there. Son, I will always love you, no matter what. But I want to know. Did you visit the meat market?"

His son looked the father in the eye and answered, "Dad, I am a McDonald. And I honored the family name."

We are *Christ*ians. It is our family name. Living within a faith-oriented system of ethics does not earn our place in the family. Rather, it reflects the fact that we have embraced and live by the family's values.

Second, discipleship is *a symbol of Thanksgiving*. If someone chooses to give me a car, I am going to write him or her a thank-you note. (Those who doubt that need only give it a try. I promise. I will send you a note.) If someone gives me a gift of any sort, I am going to respond with gratitude. If people treat me with kindness, I am going to be kind to them. If people love me, I am going to love them back. Unlike wild animals, we do not bite the hands that feed us. Instead, we shake or kiss those hands.

Discipleship is our way of sending God a thank-you note. God is gracious enough to grant us not only life eternal in the world to come but also life with meaning in this world here and now. It is something we cannot do for ourselves but that God chooses to do for us. How can we not be grateful? How better can we express our gratitude to God than by how we treat God's other creatures?

A British missionary to Uganda served for years among people who were rather unresponsive for the most part. He experienced small victories here and there (a few village churches that survived, one or two that even thrived), but mainly he worked hard under dire circumstances with small results. When asked by a journalist, "Why do you keep giving so much of yourself to people who give so little back in return?" he answered, "I love because I have been loved."

It was his way of saying that discipleship is a response to grace. God loved that missionary enough to claim him, to forgive him, and to send his own Son to live and die for him. In return, the missionary decided to pass that love along. It was his way of expressing thanks to God. "I love because I have been loved."

John's account of Jesus' post-resurrection conversation with Simon Peter illustrates the principle that discipleship follows grace. In the courtyard of Caiaphas, when it mattered most, when the chips were on the table, Peter had three times denied even knowing Jesus. According to John, he was the last person with a chance to testify for the defense. He was the final disciple remaining nearby, the only one who could speak a word on Jesus' behalf during his capital offense trial. But Peter, who earlier that evening had vainly claimed that even if all the other disciples fled, he would remain faithful, saved his own skin at Jesus' expense.

Following the resurrection, Jesus appeared by the lake while Peter and the others were fishing. In conversation after breakfast, three times Jesus asked, "Simon, son of Jonah, do you love me?" Three times, Peter answered that he did, each time eliciting from Jesus an invitation to discipleship. That invitation obviously was not based on Peter's merit. If anything, he deserved to be rejected by Christ, even as he had rejected Christ before Caiaphas. His restoration into the fellowship was purely and simply an act of grace. But it was grace married to calling. "Feed my sheep," Jesus told him (John 21:16-17). The theological model of the story indicates that Jesus calls us and accepts us in spite of our unworthiness, and we respond to him through our discipleship. We accept the fact that we have been accepted.

Virtually all Christians—liberal or conservative, high church or evangelical, Methodist, Baptist, Presbyterian, Catholic, etc.—agree that we are called to live our faith, to practice discipleship. Likewise, we all agree that living a Christian life is not what makes God love us; it is what we do because he loves us. It is a mark of our relationship with him. It is our way of saying "Thanks."

John Dear described the late Fr. Henri Nouwen as a man whose "belovedness" preceded and demanded a response of social justice and service. Dear wrote,

> What intrigues me most about Henri is that he struggled on a personal level to live [his] writings, to make the connection between his grand spiritual vision and daily, gritty reality, to put the Gospel into practice in his own life and so in the world. This struggle was painful for Henri, as it is for everyone. It meant taking risks, moving on, and seeking God's place for him in the world. A Dutch priest and psychologist, he became a popular author and speaker, as well as a favorite professor at Notre Dame, Yale and Harvard. But then, at the height of his career, he walked away from the academic world. . . . He moved to Toronto and joined the L'Arche Daybreak community to serve people who are severely disabled . . . .
>
> While many others may promote a private, comfortable, bourgeois spirituality that enjoys a privileged place as God's personal "beloved," Henri knew that all people on earth are God's beloved and that to be faithful to this belovedness means standing in solidarity with the world's suffering poor, the hungry, the marginalized, and the enemy, that we love not only our neighbors as ourselves, but that we love even our enemies, from the people of Vietnam and Nicaragua to Iraq and Afghanistan.[1]

In this passage, Dear captured the theology of discipleship as a response to grace. Note how "all people on earth are God's beloved and that to be faithful to this belovedness means standing in solidarity with the world's suffering poor, the hungry, the marginalized, and the enemy . . . ." In short, God's grace precedes our discipleship.

God loves us into loving. God accepts us into accepting. And through the mystery of the cross, a sacrifice is made on our behalf that stimulates those who are spiritually awake and alive (in Jesus' words) to "go and do likewise."

Years ago, there was a man affectionately known as "the Shoe Man of Haiti." He communicated with churches, department stores, and shoe manufacturers in America, procuring sandals and tennis shoes for the impoverished children of his country. When shipments arrived, he would put the shoes in bags and walk to remote villages to distribute them. When asked to explain his passion for that ministry, he simply answered, "When I was a barefoot child, someone gave me a pair of shoes."

Why do we seek to perform works of justice and righteousness? Virtually all Christians agree about the answer to that. We do so in response to God's grace. We love God, and we love others, "because God first loved us" (1 John 4:19).

## Note

1. From the foreword to Henri Nouwen's book *Peacework* (Maryknoll NY: Orbis Books, 2005).

## Questions for Discussion

1. If grace is unearned and unconditional, why does behavior matter?

_____

_____

_____

_____

_____

2. How does the experience of grace initiate and foster discipleship?

_____

_____

_____

_____

3. What is the relationship between "mercy" and "justice"?

_____

_____

_____

_____

4. Discuss the concepts of grace and discipleship in light of the words of Christ: "This is my commandment, that you love one another, as I have loved you" (John 13:34).

_____

_____

_____

_____

# CHAPTER 9

# THE LIFE OF PRAYER
# AND MEDITATION

Don Aycock, a Baptist pastor and writer, begins a book called *Prayer 101* by asking what the reader would do if he or she were to go to the mailbox and find this invitation in it: "Dear Friend, You are cordially invited to attend a meeting between you and God. The time is flexible, and you may accept this invitation as early as five minutes from now. Your Host is awaiting your reply. Please do not be long."[1]

That would be startling, wouldn't it? What would any of us do if we received such an invitation? Maybe, as Aycock suggests, we would check the postmark to see where the invitation had originated. But, if we took the matter seriously, wouldn't it be thrilling to know that God really did want to meet us in prayer?

In the tangle of discord and disagreements in the world over theological or practical topics in the church's life, prayer is another of the bottom line beliefs on which we all seem to agree. In my life in the ministry, I have never yet come upon a congregation anywhere that did not profess to believe in the importance of prayer as our lifeline to God.

In truth, whether you are liberal or conservative, a Primitive Baptist or a high church Anglican, Robert Tilton or John Spong, we all understand and attest that one's life of faith is undeniably strengthened by prayer and meditation. In fact, not only do virtually all Christians believe that, for the most part all people of other faiths believe it as well.

Muslims withdraw from the world five times a day and kneel toward Mecca. Jews in Jerusalem go the Wailing Wall, and practitioners of that faith everywhere wear and honor prayer shawls. Hindus meditate on the lives of the respected dead and on what they believe to be their own past lives and lives yet to come. Buddhists set aside time regularly to cloister in silence and contemplate peace and Nirvana. Ba'hais regularly meditate about the Great Truths that bind all faiths together and how many streams lead to the same ocean. And some people who practice no religion at all still center and meditate through practices like yoga or transcendental meditation.

Judging from the practices of the world's major faith traditions, there is strength to be found in practicing the discipline of prayer. Whereas praying according to format or prescription may seem to lack spontaneity or authenticity, it does immerse one in the deep faith waters of one's predecessors. Therein one often finds a sense of strength, history, and comfort.

I am blessed in my work to meet pastors and theologians of every denomination and every theological perspective, and I have found that I learn and grow from them all. Earlier in this chapter I mentioned Episcopal bishop John Spong. He is identified with the most liberal schools of faith and biblical interpretation. Some read his works and assume that he lives and operates beyond the bounds of traditional Christian thought. It is neither my intent nor my place to argue that opinion one way or the other. However, on a purely anecdotal basis, the first time my wife and I had dinner with Bishop and Mrs. Spong, when the meal was served I found myself in a dilemma. It is the practice of our family at home to join hands before a meal, to bow our heads, to thank God for what we are about to eat, and then to conclude the prayer in Jesus' name. But I was at a table with John Spong. Surely, I assumed, he didn't do things like that. Certainly his understanding of prayer could not be so conventional. Would he find it shallow or meaningless to join in our tradition? Would he silently critique it and think of me, "Poor deluded boy"? So I did something I had witnessed another clergy do at meals. I simply waved my hands above the food and said, "God knows how thankful we are for a feast like this!"

As I picked up my fork and prepared to eat, Spong, the liberal, push-the-envelope, question-the-basics theologian, said, "How interesting. Personally, I am far more comfortable with traditional prayers at mealtime. I guess it's the way I was brought up."

I was censured, but not for being too traditional in my praying. Rather, I was censured for not being traditional enough!

As stated earlier, from the pentecostal TV preacher Tilton to liberal Bishop Spong to almost everyone in between, the contemplative life is crucial, and strength is found in the practice of prayer, even (and sometimes especially) in traditional and disciplined approaches to it.

Over a quiet lunch (where I offered grace quite conventionally, by the way), Martin Marty told me of preaching in a convent in Kentucky. Throughout the sermon, he said, he heard the soft clicking of rosaries as the nuns rubbed the beads together. Far from being distracting, said Marty, it was inspiring to know that those nuns were employing the tradition of the rosary to pray for him as he stood to deliver a word from God. The ancient tradition empowered the existential experience.

It is my good fortune to know a number of wonderful young physicians who are deeply involved in church and keenly interested in faith and prayer and how that relates to their lives of science. One told me recently about studies done in three major schools of medicine. According to him, a study conducted at an Ivy League medical school indicated that people who receive medical treatment plus prayer heal more quickly and have a lower mortality rate than those who receive medical treatment without prayer.

A study was conducted at a prestigious research hospital in Maryland that indicated that the practice of prayer among patients with hypertension lowers blood pressure to normal levels during prayer and for a considerable period of time following it.

A study among cancer patients at a California university med school suggested that those who practiced religious meditation responded more effectively to chemotherapy and had a higher rate of remission and cure.

Studies such as these reveal what people of faith have believed for centuries—that prayer and meditation strengthen and enhance life as few other disciplines can.

Jesus understood that principle and practiced it. Frequently he "withdrew by himself to a lonely place" (Matt 14:13). Jesus knew he could not constantly give himself away for others without also periodically removing himself from others to take something in. You cannot press on incessantly without occasionally stopping to refuel.

We burn out when we race and rush and run and work and consistently ignore the Old Testament principle of *Shabbat*—a time of rest and reflection. From a purely practical standpoint, how can anyone possibly live a life of faith while excluding prayer and meditation?

For example, simple logic decrees that you cannot love someone while ignoring them. That principle applies to God and prayer as much as it does to interpersonal human relationships. It is illogical to claim a love for God without ever having conversations with God. And prayer is essentially that—a conversation with God.

A woman going through separation leading to divorce asked for my prayers. I replied, "What went wrong?" to which she answered, "Silence." My facial expression apparently revealed that I found this hard to interpret, so she continued, "My husband doesn't talk to me. He doesn't let me into his world. He doesn't share what's going on inside him . . . what he's happy about or worried about. Sometimes a whole day will pass, and we will be alone in the house together, and he never utters a single word. It's as if I am invisible."

If our prayer life is nothing more than "God is great and God is good" at mealtime, or "Jesus, get me out of this mess" when we are in trouble, then God is not in reality being included in our lives. We are not in conversation with him. Prayer is conversation—talking to God and listening for his reply.

Meditation is a large component of the listening part of prayer. If a person only talks, then he or she is not involved in a conversation. Merely talking is a monologue. Conversing includes listening to the other person, learning from them, taking them seriously, and thinking about what they have to say and how it applies to your life.

It is especially essential to *think* about what they have to say. You cannot learn a discipline without thinking it through. I would never have learned to balance my checkbook if some teacher in a math class years ago had not made me think about adding and subtracting. I would never have learned to drive a car if some instructor in a drivers' ed class years ago had not made me think about motor vehicle operation and safety.

An incredibly successful motivational speaker was asked by a news reporter how he had managed to reach his level of fame. He answered, "Someone taught me that I should envision what I wanted to become. When I could see it, I could claim it. And when I claimed it, I became it."

I do not entirely buy into that philosophy. I can envision myself as a great singer or the point guard for the Detroit Pistons, but there is no way I'll ever attain those goals. Yet, at a deeper level, the speaker had something to say that most of us need to hear.

If, for example, I am having health problems, quiet meditation upon the state of my body can produce benefits. If I envision myself as healthy, it inspires me to do the things required to become healthy, whatever those things may be. For one person it may mean adopting a more reasonable diet; for another, increasing exercise; for another, giving up alcohol or tobacco.

If I meditate about personal relationships, the process itself causes me to think about what I need to do to make those relationships strong. For one person, that may mean asking someone to forgive them; for another, it may mean restructuring their schedule to spend more time with those who are important; for another, it may mean learning to be a better listener.

As Christians, few things offer us a deeper experience of meaningful life than meditation on key questions: What does God want of me? What do I want from life? Why am I here? What important things am I missing because I am so busy with lesser things? What am I going to do about it? People who do not think long and seriously about those questions basically sleepwalk their way through life and miss real living in the process.

We may argue and debate about a million issues large and small, but one topic on which virtually all serious Christians agree is *the inexpressible value of the life of prayer*: how (emotionally, relationally, physically, and spiritually) prayer and meditation do things for us that nothing else can do. If we do not practice them, we cheat our own lives.

Corrie Ten Boom, in relating her dark days imprisoned in a Nazi war camp, claimed that the practice of prayer and personal meditation saved her life. During the long nights of hunger and suffering, she said, her prayers and thoughts of God would lift her from her confines. She felt transported to a safe haven where God's arms held and protected her. In that place her strength was renewed, and she found the power to face again the tests and trials of the coming day.[2]

She was not referring to astral projection or any other New Age idea. She was speaking of the soul, the inner and essential self that, by communing with God, could be lifted above the perils of the particular moment and could experience peace. In fact, given the conditions in which she lived, she found "peace that passes understanding" (Phil 4:7).

Catholics call it "the contemplative life." Whatever title is bestowed, directed prayers and meditation spiritually and emotionally transport us to a place where we experience divine presence. And in that presence, there is peace.

## Notes

1. Don Aycock, *Prayer 101: Learning to Talk with God* (Atlanta: Chalice Press, 2007).

2. Corrie Ten Boom, *The Hiding Place* (New York: Random House, 1982).

# Questions for Discussion

1. Discuss the idea of prayer as "Shabbat."

_____

_____

_____

_____

_____

2. How might prayer be an experience of listening?

_____

_____

_____

_____

_____

3. In what ways might personal meditation affect one's behavior?

_____

_____

_____

_____

_____

4. How might prayer and meditiation be part of a *physically* healthy lifestyle? Explain your response.

_____

_____

_____

_____

_____

# CHAPTER 10

# SACRAMENTS

The word "sacrament" is taken from the Latin *sacramentum,* which literally means "an oath of allegiance" or "an obligation." The root is *sacrare*: "to consecrate." The Christian church in the early centuries of its existence borrowed the idea of *sacrare* and used it to designate certain liturgical acts or religious rites that the church felt were divinely consecrated. Those acts were considered to be means of grace, moments in which God's presence and accepting love broke through in some mysterious way that could neither be explained nor denied.

Throughout the centuries, different communities of believers have considered a variety of religious rites as being sacramental in nature. In Roman Catholicism, for example, seven specific rites are deemed sacramental (Baptism, Confirmation, Communion, Penance and Reconciliation, Anointing the sick, Holy Orders, and Matrimony). In some churches, there are two sacraments and five special orders. Other fellowships consider acts such as last rites to be sacramental. Others include in their lists various observances from christening to foot-washing. Most mainline Protestant churches recognize two sacraments: baptism and Communion.

The point is that amid our differences in determining what acts are in fact sacramental, there is a bottom line belief among all Christians that certain corporate activities are signs of grace, detectible by the senses, and able to make us aware of God's presence and love in ways both actual and symbolic.

For purposes of theological exploration only, let's consider two acts: baptism and Communion. That is not to say those are the only sacraments. Rather, by wrestling with a couple of sacramental concepts, we can experience the mystery and multiple interpretive possibilities of them all.

## Baptism

Baptism is practiced by virtually all Christian denominations, but in a wide variety of ways. Some churches require immersion. Others permit pouring or sprinkling (a variation of pouring). Some churches require additional baptisms each time you join a different congregation, or encourage re-baptisms each time a person makes a new spiritual commitment. Others contend that baptism, as an act of God, is a once-and-for-all-time experience. When God accepts us, he accepts us. He extends the grace of the sacrament correctly the first time, and it needs no correction or reapplication in the future.

Some churches confuse the sacrament of baptism with the ritual of christening (which is simply the liturgical observance of giving a child a name). Some churches baptize only persons who have reached an age of accountability and are able to make a profession of faith. Baptism, thus, becomes the liturgical act that seals the person's profession. Other churches practice infant baptism, theologically contending that baptism is God's act of accepting us, not vice versa, and thus is not restricted to persons who make public professions or accept prescribed dogmas. Biblically, there is no certain ground to occupy in the various debates.

In response to the Philippian jailer's question, "What must I do to be saved?" Paul advised, "Repent and believe," after which the man and his whole family were baptized (Acts 16:30-33). In that story is a formula indicating that repentance precedes profession of faith, which precedes baptism. It is also noteworthy that there is the implication that in that culture, the conversion of the head of the house brought all the family members into the church (whether or not they desired such). The jailer professed faith, whereupon he and all his house were baptized. Be that as it may, the formula is clear: repentance, profession of faith, baptism.

However, when one reads the story of Jesus' own baptism, the formula is reversed. The first Gospel writer, Mark, devotes a significant portion of the first chapter of his book to the baptism of Jesus. In that account, Jesus does nothing but show up. The movement is from top down, from God to person, not from person to God.

Jesus goes to the river where he receives baptism. The heavens open, and a dove descends and lands upon him—a symbol of God's Spirit bestowed upon the man Jesus. Then a voice is heard from heaven, saying, "This is my beloved Son, with whom I am well pleased" (Mark 1:11). To that point, Jesus has neither said nor done a thing. No act of repentance. No profession of faith. All the movement is from top down. God is the actor, and Jesus is the recipient.

Following that, says Mark, Jesus is driven into the wilderness to be tempted by Satan for forty days. At the end of that period, "Jesus came into Galilee, preaching the gospel of God" (Mark 1:14).

At baptism, Jesus realized that God had accepted and claimed him for a sacred purpose. In the wilderness, Jesus wrestled with that knowledge. He was tempted physically (to turn stones into bread), religiously (to throw himself from the temple and demonstrate his miraculous gifts), and politically (to worship Satan and be given power over the kingdoms of this world). If the temptations were not real, the entire passage is pointless. If they were real, then at that point Jesus was still struggling to determine whether to accept the fact that he had been accepted. In Mark's story, baptism precedes commitment.

"So," one might ask, "which method is right?" The answer is "Both." The New Testament is not didactic about the methodology of baptism. It seems that baptism can be either a sign of one's faith or a prelude to it, a sign of conversion or of God's claim upon those who are not yet converted. The point is that, however one interprets it, baptism is a significant symbol of one's spiritual journey, despite the fact that to different people it represents different stops on the journey.

### Communion (also called the Eucharist and the Lord's Supper)

Across the years, discussion and often debate has existed about what actually happens during the service of Communion. Are the elements (bread and wine) literally transformed into the real body and blood of Christ?

An ancient doctrine (dating back to AD 1079 and first articulated by Hildebert de Lavardin, Archbishop of Tours) was called "transubstantiation." It taught that after being consecrated (*sacrare*), the priest was literally distributing blood and body. The substance had been transformed into something entirely different—from yeast and dough to flesh, from fermented grape juice to blood. Priests were even required to drink the wine that remained after a service (after all, one cannot casually pour the blood of Christ down a sink). There was also a song to be sung while placing the bread back into its container. The song was titled "Putting Jesus to Bed."

A more moderate position, especially articulated within denominations that were the offspring of the Reformation, was called "consubstantiation" and was preached by such persons as Martin Luther. He believed that whereas the substance of the elements remained bread and wine, the essence was transformed into body and blood.

Others, such as Huldrych Zwingli, believed and taught that the bread and wine were simply symbols of the body and blood of Christ, reminding us of his sacrifice, but in no substantial or essential way anything other than dough and juice.

In a post-modern era, most Christians seem underwhelmed by the whole debate. Even within Catholic circles, few appear to hitch their theological wagons to "transubstantiation," and most believers have migrated to Zwingli's camp.

Another point of disagreement, if not debate, revolves around whether or not Communion is even a biblical concept. The service reportedly dates back to Christ's experience with his disciples in the upper room. Shortly before his betrayal, Jesus blessed bread and wine and distributed it to his friends, saying, "This is my body (blood), given (shed) for you" (Luke 22:19-20). That, say many, is when Communion began. In that moment Jesus instituted a new sacramental service for the church.

Before summarily accepting that point of view, one needs to remember two things. First, at that point, there was no Christian church. It simply did not exist. Sometime later, following Pentecost, it was born and simply called "the Way." When Jesus met with his disciples in the upper room, there was no church for which to institute a new service.

The second thing to remember is that Jesus and his disciples were in that room to observe the Passover meal. It was the traditional Jewish Seder. Jesus assumed the role of the father on those occasions, answering the standard Seder questions, blessing the food, and telling the children when to eat. It was all didactic and instructional. At one point, Jesus said, "Do this in remembrance of me" (Luke 22:19). And what were his disciples to "do"? They were to observe the Passover meal, and in their future observances, they were to remember the last time they had that meal with Jesus and the sacrifice he proceeded to make for them. They were to mentally connect the Passover lamb with the "Pascal Lamb" (meaning Christ). It was not the institution of a new sacrament. It was, instead, an addition of new meaning to an old observance.

One may ask, "What, then, of the holy meals to which Paul refers in Corinthians? Surely by that time, church people received Communion." In the early days of "the Way," Christians met together in homes for worship. They ordinarily did so at the end of a workday. Food was provided. They ate the evening meal together, after which those in attendance worshiped by singing psalms, praying prayers, and remembering aloud the deeds and teachings of Jesus. Worship began *after* the meal was concluded. The meal itself was not incorporated into the worship event, but was much like the family night potluck dinners that precede a revival service.

When Paul chastised the people in Corinth about their behavior at the sacred meal, he said that too many people arrived early for the fellowship meals, ate all the food, and sometimes got drunk from the wine before some people even had a chance to show up! When they did, there was nothing left with which to feed the rest of the crowd (1 Cor 11:18-29). In short, Paul chastised the church in Corinth about table manners, not about sacramentalism. To be sure, in this pericope he did give us our traditional words of institution (vv. 23-25), but he did not indicate, nor does the New Testament elsewhere indicate, that there existed at that time an organized liturgical service similar to what we know as the Eucharist. Indeed, the service of Communion seems to have been a creation of the institutional church but not of the Bible itself.

So what do we do with it? The response is that we do not deify it. Nor do we dictate how it must be observed to be authentic. If it is a creation of church rather than Scripture, then it is the property of the various cultures and practices of a wide array of churches.

I have had staff members who were Episcopalians and Disciples of Christ, all of whom said to me that they "needed" Communion every week. Worship did not meet their needs without it.

The pastor of an 18,000-member major Protestant congregation said to me, "If I were never to receive or celebrate Communion again, I wouldn't miss it much." He is a deeply spiritual man with a strong commitment to God and church. He is simply not a high church liturgist, and his needs are fed via means other than the Eucharist.

I grew up in a traditional Protestant church in the South. We observed the Lord's Supper four times a year. It was our tradition, our norm, and so to me that has always felt natural and adequate. Unlike my former staff members, I do not sense a need for weekly Communion. Unlike my friend who serves the large church, I do sense a need for occasional Communion (and cannot imagine Christmas Eve or Maundy Thursday without it). Who is right? Who is wrong? The answer is that there is no right or wrong.

Communion is a means of grace, and as such it ministers to different people in entirely different ways.

In truth, regardless of denomination, most people care less for theological debate than for existential experience. The questions have become, "In what ways do these services affect me?" "Am I different because of receiving baptism or Communion?" "Does it matter in my life?"

Sacraments matter as symbols of that to which they point. "This do in remembrance of me." The sacraments point us toward a deeper reality, the reality of God's claim upon our lives and his unconditional, even sacrificial love for us.

In my office I keep something I call my "Sunshine File." It is a collection of letters, cards, and e-mails in which someone offered unexpected (usually undeserved) affirmation or love. In everyone's life come times of darkness and shadow. When those moments come for me, I turn to my file and find sunshine again.

The file itself is a cardboard box with bits of paper folded and stored. But each bit of paper is a reminder of something more—of grace, of goodness, of human kindness, and of healing love. I can look at the box, and it reminds me of those qualities. I can read the notes, and each one symbolizes a real, live, flesh-and-blood individual whose mercy restores my soul. Neither the box nor the papers within it are sacred in and of themselves, but they point toward people who are.

Sacraments are services that point toward the One who is sacred, reminding us of his grace and goodness and kindness and healing love. They are liturgical sunshine files; not the Light, but vessels through which the Light illumines our darkness.

## Questions for Discussion

1. Discuss the difference between "believers' baptism" and baptism solely as an act of God's grace.

_____

_____

_____

_____

_____

2. What do you think takes place in the moment of baptism? What might be the results of receiving that sacrament?

_____

_____

_____

_____

_____

3. Discuss the difference between transubstantiation, consubstantiation, and Communion as a service of symbol and remembrance.

_____

_____

_____

_____

_____

4. In what ways might the Eucharist affect the nature of fellowship within a local congregation?

_____

_____

_____

_____

_____

# CHAPTER 11

# ECCLESIOLOGY

The word *ecclesiology* refers to the study of the nature of the church. Virtually every Christian believes that church is important. Not all agree about what kind of church or about what level of support they give to it.

On Christmas and Easter Sundays, for example, almost every Christian church in the world is packed to the rafters with people who have come to worship. I am always tempted on those Sundays either to say (a) "You know, we plan to do this again next week if you want to come," or (b) to quote the late Clovis Chappell, who said from his pulpit the Sunday before Christmas, "Some of you have put on a little weight since Easter!"

Traditionally, the Sundays following Christianity's key celebrative days of faith are called "low Sundays." On those days, church people tend to develop ecclesiaphobia (fear of church), or at least homiliphobia (fear of sermons). While there is no consensus about the importance of a level of participation or support, virtually all Christians still agree that church, in some fashion, is undeniably important.

In the early ages of Christianity, three major schools of thought dominated the theological landscape regarding how a person is "saved." One school of thought was *soteria sola gratia* (salvation by grace alone). Another was *soteria sola fides* (salvation by faith alone).

But a third school, equally important and perhaps larger in number than the other two, was *soteria sola ecclesia* (salvation through the church alone). In the early days of Christianity, a predominant belief was that you could not achieve salvation (which, remember, biblically means "to be made whole") outside of the church.

In fact, for centuries Christian theologians taught a doctrine called "extended incarnation," meaning that God's Spirit was first made flesh, or "incarnate," in Jesus, and afterward his Spirit was made incarnate in the church. The church, they taught, was the ongoing, living reality of Christ. That idea was taken from Paul, who said to the Christians in Corinth, "Now, you are the Body of Christ, and individually members of it" (1 Cor 12:27).

Historically, for almost two thousand years Christians have believed that church is indispensable to our experience of God and life of faith.

Somewhere along the line (in the latter half of the twentieth century), that changed. In Europe today, roughly 10 percent of all people attend church. Church is considered a social gathering for the elite but not a home for the masses. In America, whereas just over 90 percent of our people say they believe in God, less than 40 percent ever go to any church anywhere at any time (as noted earlier, with the possible exceptions of Christmas and Easter).

The turning point in America was the Viet Nam War and the subsequent death of institutional loyalty. Until that time, our national sentiment had been, "My country right or wrong, but still my country!" After Viet Nam, Americans were no longer so trusting. They felt they had been lied to. They had been asked to buy into something that the majority of Americans felt should never have happened. From that time on, the American public has said, "Prove to me that you can be trusted, and prove to me that you deserve my support!"

That posture is clearly visible through public opinion polls revealing Americans' lack of support for military involvement in Iraq. Whatever your politics, you cannot deny that the vast majority of Americans no longer blindly accept political actions unless those actions can be demonstrably validated. Since Viet Nam, not merely Missouri but all the other forty-nine states as well have become "show me" states.

That same death of institutional loyalty has affected the church. There was a time when denominational loyalists said (fill in the name of whatever denomination you choose), "I'm _____ born and _____ bred, And when I die, I'll be _____ dead!" That ended forty years ago. People no longer sign on with an institution for life. Instead, they say, "Prove to me that you deserve my loyalty. Show me!"

Add to that the fact that we have become a mobile nation. The average American family changes houses every two years. Instead of growing up in the same little community, buying a piece of property a half mile from their parents' house, and going to the same church from the cradle to the grave, now people live in one city for four years, then move to the next for two, then to the next for six, then the next for ten, then back home to retire. In every one of those towns, they no longer look for a church of their denomination. Remember, institutional loyalty is no longer a primary factor in individual decision-making. Instead, people look for a church that meets their needs.

As Herb Miller suggests in his book *How to Build a Magnetic Church*,[1] when it comes to finding a church, people no longer care about what's on the sign on the lawn. Instead, they care about what's going on inside the building! And if nothing much is going on, they will keep looking, or else they will stop looking altogether and practice faith in private, personal, and unchurched ways.

Therefore, in order to thrive, and sometimes merely in order to survive, a local church has to do several things. No longer do people think the only way to God is through holy doors. No longer does anyone seem to believe in *soteria sola ecclesia*—salvation only though the church. Thus, people will come through the doors of a church only if we on the inside do a few things faithfully and well.

One of those things is to *talk about faith*. That is what we do and who we are. In the sixties and seventies, many quit talking so much about faith and began talking almost exclusively about social issues. They are important and not to be ignored. But in church, our consideration of the great issues facing society always has to be framed in the context of faith itself. Otherwise, we become a social services agency or a political activist group, and the world already has a lot of those. In the eighties and nineties, many churches talked primarily about pop psychology. Again, psychology is an important discipline, but in the setting of a church it must be discussed as part of faith exploration and not as a substitute for it.

The senior pastor of one of America's largest TV congregations ordered his trustees to remove all crosses from the church. He did not want anyone to see a cross when they tuned into his TV worship service. Why? Because, he said, crosses make people think of evil and suffering, and he wanted his television audience to think positive, encouraging, uplifting thoughts instead. He substituted self-help, pop psychology for Christian theology.

Throughout all the years of people trying to substitute secular stories for *the Story*, mainline Protestantism continued to decline. Church sociologists such as Herb Miller, Lyle Schaller, and George Barna have found that churches that grow are churches that talk about faith. You go to a grocery store to find food and to a library to find books. People come to a church to hear about religion, and the local church ought not to be shy about it.

Churches survive and even thrive when they *provide opportunities for people to practice discipleship.* Church growth experts consistently agree (basing their opinion on surveys conducted since the beginning of membership decline in traditional Protestant denominations more than forty years ago) that rarely does the health of a congregation depend on location, the strengths of the pastor, or the attractiveness of the building. Instead, the key factor that draws people to church is how a congregation answers the question, "Can I do something in or through this place that will make a difference in the world?" If the answer is yes, then people sign on with the church. If the answer is no, they simply join the Lions Club or the Civitans.

Jesus instructed his followers to "Let your light so shine before others that, seeing your good works, they give glory to God" (Matt 5:16). Years ago I served a suburban church that maintained a constant, rarely fluctuating membership. Though the area around the church was growing, the congregation itself remained static. In a church leadership meeting, the question was asked why such a church in such a location, with a beautiful facility, failed to grow. A member of the congregation stood to respond. He said, "What are we famous for?" No one ventured an answer, perhaps because they didn't understand the question, so he continued. "When people think of our church, what comes to mind? I'll tell you," he said. "They think of chicken pies. We have the best chicken pie suppers in the county. People drive from neighboring counties to eat here or to carry home pies to serve their families. You can ask anyone in the city, and they will tell you that we are famous for chicken pies. But," he concluded, "though people will drive here to eat, no one wants to join a church that is merely famous for chicken!"

The man clearly articulated an irrefutable truth about what attracts people to churches. It is not the architecture, or the pastor, or even the music or location or chicken pies. People are attracted to churches that are famous for making a difference in the world, for allowing individuals to practice discipleship and do something that adds value to life. "Let your light so shine before others that, *seeing your good works*, they give glory to God."

Finally, people want to *experience God*, and most of them still believe church is the most likely place for that to happen. Julia Augustine operates a food and housing shelter for abused women in Los Angeles. More than a hundred women come there each day, most of them sent by the police under protective custody. Every day Julia arranges for them to receive medical care, clothing, transportation to and from work, and a safe place to sleep. Every day she listens to them as long as they need to talk.

Julia said that across her years in that work, she has discovered something interesting. The most frequent question she hears is not, "Why did he do this to me?" but rather, "Do you think there is someone out there who will actually love me?" Among those women who have suffered inexpressible abuse, she said, the primary question is not about their abusers who hurt them but rather about the possibility of a personal being who will love them. Julia responds by sharing the story of Someone out there who loves them and who demonstrated that love via the promise, "I will be with you always" (Matt 28:20).

So it is for us all. At the end of the day, we want to know if there is Someone out there who will love us and hear us and accept us and forgive us and help us find meaning in life. And it does not really matter if yours is a Methodist church or a Baptist church, a Catholic church or a Lutheran church, a liberal church or a Pentecostal church. People come to churches seeking God. It is a basic hunger we all have in common, whatever our denomination may be.

Even a cursory glance at global history reveals the wonderful enhancement of human life that is directly attributable to the work of the church. Every local community can report countless positive effects resulting from the presence and work of that community's congregations. Public policies ranging from child welfare to women's rights to civil rights have been transformed, among other reasons, because of the moral voice of church people who stood tall and stood fast. But a postmodern "show me" culture no longer embraces any institution based merely on its legacy. For the church to remain viable in contemporary culture, it has to produce.

One of the bottom line beliefs of all Christians is the importance of the institution of the church as a place where faith is explored, where discipleship is practiced, and where God is made available to us all. And one of the bottom line challenges, especially within American and Western European churches, is for its adherents to become proponents—actively doing what is required to make the church of the future as transformational, relevant, and vibrant as was the Christian institution described on the pages of world history.

The late Bishop Ernest Fitzgerald told of a church building in New York City that had a "for sale" sign on the front lawn. The grass had grown almost knee high. Many of the beautiful stained-glass windows were broken and covered with boards. Large chains kept the massive oak doors fastened together.

Beside the "for sale" sign on the church lawn, someone had placed another sign. It was handwritten and proclaimed this message to all its passersby: "This church went out of business because it forgot what its business was."

Our business is to discuss faith, to practice love, and to provide a place where people can experience God. When churches remember their business, lives and communities touched by those churches are transformed.

## Note

1. Herb Miller, *How to Build a Magnetic Church*, Creative Leadership Series (Nashville: Abingdon, 1987).

# Questions for Discussion

1. Why might early Church theologians have espoused the idea of "*Soteria* [salvation, wholeness] *Sola Ecclesia*"?

_____

_____

_____

_____

_____

2. Discuss the ancient idea of "extended incarnation." Does that concept have any relevance today?

_____

_____

_____

_____

_____

3. Do you think denominationalism is dead in the Western world? Explain your response.

_____

_____

_____

_____

_____

4. What are the benefits of involvement in a faith community? How does society benefit? How do individuals benefit?

_____

_____

_____

_____

_____

# CHAPTER 12

# LIFE AFTER DEATH

Some time ago the football team of the university in the city where I live played in the Orange Bowl in Miami, Florida. It was an exciting time for our whole city, a time filled with celebration and hope. Though I am a graduate of a different university, this was still the team from "my town." I am friends with faculty and administrative personnel. I sometimes preach in their chapel. I go to the stadium and watch those athletes play. I have become an "adopted fan." Thus, I shared in the city's disappointment when, in the end, we came up short.

In truth, our team should have won. They suffered three turnovers in the red zone, two fumbles and an interception, all of which should have been touchdowns. Television replays indicated that two of the turnovers appeared to result from questionable calls by officials. That made the pill even more difficult to swallow. Arguably, our team outplayed and should have defeated the team that wound up number four in the nation.

The next day, a friend said, "I hope everyone considers the bright side." Asked what that might be, he replied, "First, they won the conference championship. Second, they won more games this season than any football team in the university's history. Third, their coach was named the national Coach of the Year. Fourth, except for their opponent, all the other football teams in America were home watching on television. At least they made the dance, and that's quite an accomplishment. And fifth, they have sixteen starters returning next year, which means another big year could be on the horizon. They could have a resurrection!"

My friend, using football as an analogy, spoke theologically. He described the pains and beauties of mortal living, the victories and setbacks, all framed within the irrepressible hope of resurrection. A bottom line belief shared by virtually every Christian denomination in the world is belief in life beyond this life. That belief is based, to a great extent, on the biblical witness.

Part of that witness was the testimony of Christ. Jesus said, "And I, if I be lifted up, shall draw all others unto myself" (John 12:32). And again, "I am the resurrection and the life. Whoever believes in me, though he were dead, yet shall he live. And whosoever lives and believes in me shall never die" (John 11:25).

Of course, some retort, "Anyone can say anything. Just because a man once promised a resurrection doesn't mean that it actually occurred." But our bottom line belief has a ready response to that. Not only were words spoken that predicted the resurrection, but afterward there were the numerous resurrection appearances of Christ—to Mary in the garden, to the travelers on the road to Emmaus, to the disciples in a locked room and later beside the sea, and finally to a significant number of persons at the Mount of the Ascension. Add to that the assertion of Paul that he could name five hundred people who had seen Jesus after the resurrection. As noted in chapter 3, it is hard to get five hundred people to share the same hallucination or tell the same lie.

So virtually every Christian denomination in the world believes and teaches that Jesus was raised from the dead, and therefore his followers shall be, too.

Not every individual Christian believes that. Many practicing Christians are more-or-less early Old Testament Hebrews in their interpretation of life beyond death. In the early days of Judaism people believed that *one lives on after death only through progeny*, through the memories of one's offspring. That is why they considered barrenness a curse. Without children and grandchildren to remember you, at death you simply ceased to exist. A few persons within Christian congregations concur. They believe that you live this life, and when it is over the only things that live on are what you were, did, and stood for. Thus it is imperative to make a good mark in this life because that's all that is left when the mortician closes the lid.

When some respond by appealing to the phenomenon of near-death experiences (and persons who report being drawn toward a light), skeptics argue that those are simply brain synapses that naturally occur as the body shuts down, and that the images people see of heaven or loved ones are just "comfort memories."

Traditionalists respond that it is difficult for a two-year-old, for example, to report a "comfort memory" associated with dying since two-year-olds have no concept of death. And yet, resuscitated small children frequently make those reports. Traditionalists also argue that brain synapses cannot account for the countless persons who, during clinical death on an operating table prior to resuscitation, report that their souls were lifted out of their bodies and proceed to describe accurately everything that was going on in the operating room or even in the hall outside.

Still, some individuals within Christian congregations believe much as did the early Hebrews—that life ends with death, and beyond that you live on only in your legacy or reputation. However, though various individuals within the Christian community may believe that, virtually every denomination teaches otherwise. Faith families, whether fundamentalist or liberal, tend to agree that beyond this life there is another life of some sort.

Roman Catholics and some Orthodox faiths believe in *a multifaceted understanding of life after death.* To use their language, if a person "loves God perfectly," he or she goes directly to heaven. If they love God but with obvious imperfections, they spend time in purgatory where they are "purged" of those imperfections and then sent on to heaven. If they have lived a totally depraved life and have rejected God and faith and thus died in utter sin, they are condemned to hell or extinction.

Conservative Christians believe in *a two-tiered afterlife*. A person who is "saved" will die and go to heaven, to live forever in a state of grace and in the presence of God. A person who is "unsaved" will die and go to hell, suffering forever not only for his sins but for his rejection of the grace of Christ.

Another movement within conservative Christianity believes in *a one-tiered afterlife*. They are called "Christadelphians" (lovers of Christ). Since the late 1800s, Christadelphians have been split into two schools of thought. One says that those who are "saved" die and immediately go to heaven. Those who are "unsaved" die and simply cease to exist. The second school of thought says that everyone dies, and at the Second Coming everyone is resurrected. Those who are "saved" go to heaven to be with God. Those who are "unsaved" are annihilated and simply cease to exist. Those who never heard the gospel will not be raised up at all at the Second Coming.

Of course, there are also Christians who are heavily influenced by eastern thought and believe in (a) *transportation* or (b) *reincarnation*. The former means that when you die, if your soul has unfinished work to do on earth, you are transported into an unborn fetus that has already been conceived, and you are born all over again as another human being. The latter means that you are re-created. Your soul enters a kind of "holding cell," more or less like the Hebrew Sheol, until someone conceives, and then your soul is placed in that fetus. Those who believe in reincarnation, of course, believe that in future lives our souls may be placed in other living creatures as well as human beings.

There is a debate among some Christians about *when* the soul makes its journey to heaven or hell. The predominant belief is in the immediate migration of the soul. That is, as soon as we die here, we are born on the other side. To support this belief, people quote Jesus' words to the dying criminal on the cross: "Truly I say to you, *this day* you will be with me in Paradise" (Luke 23:43).

Another school of thought called Adventism, found most notably in the Seventh Day Adventist Church, believes in what is called the General Resurrection. That doctrine, simply put, is that after death all will sleep until the Second Coming, at which time everyone will be raised, and Jesus will "separate the sheep from the goats." The sheep (i.e., the faithful) he will welcome into heaven, and the goats (the unfaithful) will be condemned to hell or extinction (Matt 25:32-33). To support their beliefs, Adventists appeal to the same verse that Jesus spoke on the cross. The difference is in how they emphasize the words: "Truly I say to you *this day*, you will be with me in Paradise."

Bottom line: We vary widely and sometimes wildly on what we believe the afterlife will be like, how we get there, when we get there, and even who gets there. But every Christian denomination agrees and teaches, to quote Paul, that "when this earthly tent we dwell in is destroyed, we have a house not made with hands, eternal in the heavens" (2 Cor 5:1). That belief is based on our trust in the wisdom and grace of God, and our belief that C. S. Lewis was correct when he suggested that God did not create his greatest treasure only, in the end, to destroy it.

In the first church I served following graduation from seminary, I visited one night with an aging woman in the hospital. She was facing serious surgery the next day. Without the surgery she would die. But the procedure was intricate and risky, and given her age and some compromising health issues, she had at best a fifty-fifty chance of surviving the operation. I went to her room expecting to find someone struggling with debilitating fear. Instead, I found a woman who seemed totally peaceful. She was smiling. Her Bible, a novel, and several pictures of her children and grandchildren sat by her bed. After a few minutes of chit chat, I cut to the chase and said, "You must be afraid as you face tomorrow." I will never forget her answer: "No, Michael, I am not at all afraid. I have lived as a Christian long enough to figure something out. If I survive, God will be with me. If I do not survive, I will be with God. Either way, I win."

However much we may argue and debate about the whats and hows, all Christian denominations stand together on the bottom line—that when this life is over, we begin a new life in a new world where there is no sickness, no sadness, and no death. So, by God's grace, whether in this world or the world to come, we win.

Not only does that belief become an antidote to fear as we face our own mortality, as in the case of the woman facing surgery, but it is likewise a powerful aid in coping with grief. How many of us have said goodbye to loved ones in the sure and certain confidence that their best lives are only beginning? A belief in life beyond this life gives individuals the capacity to survive primary losses and move forward with life.

Some years ago there appeared in an issue of *The Sanctuary for Lent* the story of a woman who lost her son to a terminal illness. She wrote of finding the power to continue life after her tragic loss only because of her confidence that her son "was not gone, but had merely gone on ahead, risen with Mary's Son who defeated death for all."

Perhaps parents of murdered children in Northern Ireland survive because of that faith. Perhaps parents who lost their children when a tornado struck a high school in Alabama do the same. Perhaps parents of slain students from Columbine to Virginia Tech do likewise. Because Mary's Son defeated death for everyone, their children, far from being "gone," have simply "gone on ahead."

When for a while the center of Christianity lay not in Rome but in Constantinople, the Eastern orthodox translation of the word "Easter" meant "God's laughter." God, through the risen Messiah, had laughed in the face of death. Death was no match for his power and was almost comical in its feeble efforts to derail him.

An ancient legend about Lazarus, the man whom Jesus raised from the dead in the Fourth Gospel, was that the Roman powers were threatened by his influence. Calling him in, the wicked Emperor Calligula demanded that he publicly refute his faith. When Lazarus refused, Calligula sought to impress upon him the seriousness of the moment. He told him that, should he continue to resist their commands, he would be put to death. Hearing that, Lazarus laughed.

Eugene O'Neill took the title of his 1925 play, *Lazarus Laughed,* from this legend. Lazarus laughed because death was no longer a threat to him. He had been there, and, because of Christ's power that was far greater than the emperor's, he had victoriously returned.[1]

A bottom line belief of most Christians is our confidence that beyond this world is another world. Beyond this mortal life is life eternal. And death is merely the portal through which we pass to that life in that world.

Natalie Sleeth's beloved "Hymn of Promise" says it so well.

In our end is our beginning;
In our time, infinity;
In our doubt there is believing;
In our life, eternity.
In our death, a resurrection;
At the last, a victory,
Unrevealed until its season,
Something God alone can see.[2]

## Notes

1. Eugene O'Neill, *Lazarus Laughed* (New York: Boni & Liveright, 1927).

2. Natalie Sleeth, "Hymn of Promise" (Carol Stream IL: Hope Publishing Company, 1938).

## Questions for Discussion

1. What do you think happens to a person at the moment of death? Why do you believe that?

_____

_____

_____

_____

_____

2. Discuss the phenomenon of "life after life" (clinical death and resuscitation) reports. How do you interpret those accounts?

_____

_____

_____

_____

_____

3. How does the biblical story of Easter affect the reality and resolution of grief?

_____

_____

_____

_____

_____

4. Do you believe in a personally aware existence following death? If not, explain your response. If so, describe your concept of what that existence might be like.

_____

_____

_____

_____